TRUTH AND FALLACY
IN
EDUCATIONAL THEORY

by

CHARLES D. HARDIE

Assistant to the Professor of Education, University of Edinburgh
formerly Bye-Fellow of Magdalene College, Cambridge

CAMBRIDGE
AT THE UNIVERSITY PRESS
1942

CONTENTS

v

PREFACE

I wish to express my warmest thanks to Professor Godfrey H. Thomson, who has not only read most of the book in manuscript but has also been a continual source of encouragement to me. My obligations to my former teachers, Professor C. D. Broad and Dr I. A. Richards, will be obvious to anyone who knows their work, and I make grateful acknowledgment to them here. My thanks are also due to the staff of the Cambridge University Press for their care and courtesy, and to Messrs Macmillan and Company, Limited, for permission to use a number of quotations from the works of John Dewey.

C. D. H.

August 1941

INTRODUCTION

The present state of educational theory, with its numerous conflicting doctrines, can hardly be regarded as satisfactory, and the present book is an attempt to resolve some of the disagreements. It has been customary to consider that disagreement in such a subject is quite respectable, just as it has long been considered to be respectable in philosophical theory. But recent years have seen a change in the attitude of some professional philosophers. The Cambridge analytical school, led by Moore, Broad and Wittgenstein, has attempted so to analyse propositions that it will always be apparent whether the disagreement between philosophers is one concerning matters of fact, or is one concerning the use of words, or is, as is frequently the case, a purely emotive one.

It is time, I think, that a similar attitude became common in the field of educational theory. That is, if two educational theorists disagree I think it should be made clear whether the disagreement is factual or verbal or due to some emotional conflict. If this is to be done it is necessary always to state each theory in the clearest possible way so that no ambiguity may be allowed to flourish undiscovered.

In the succeeding pages I have attempted to do this for what are perhaps the three most typical theories of education that have so far been proposed—the 'nature' theory of education, the theory of the development of character by means of instruction, and the theory of education by means of the practical situations of life. Each of these is examined, and in the fourth chapter an attempt is made to analyse the foundations on which any educational theory must be built. It is then possible to see to what extent disagreements may legitimately be allowed. Finally, in Chapter v an account is given of the logical assumptions involved in recent work on educational measurement.

CHAPTER I

Education According to Nature

Many educationists have held a view which they have expressed in some such words as 'a child ought to be educated according to Nature'. These educationists have often disagreed among themselves and each of them has generally used the word 'Nature' in more than one sense. Consequently, in this chapter I shall not attempt to expound the views of any one of these educationists, nor shall I attempt to expound a view which may have been common to a number of them. Rather I shall attempt to discuss a number of propositions all of which have at one time or another been held to be implied by the proposition, 'a child ought to be educated according to Nature'. I shall not consider whether the propositions actually are implied by this latter proposition, but shall consider them solely on their own merits. I do this for three reasons. First, the proposition 'a child ought to be educated according to Nature' is so vague that it is not important to decide what it implies. Secondly, the propositions which I shall consider have generally been advanced with the intention of making clear the meaning of 'a child ought to be educated according to Nature'. Thirdly, the propositions, if true, are important at the present time.

The first proposition which I wish to consider is the following: 'A child's education ought to be such that it is free to develop according to the laws of its own nature.'[1] There is a sense in which this is certainly true, the sense, namely, in which we would be continuously confronted with a series of miracles if the child did not develop according to the laws of its own nature. But in this sense the proposition, although true, is trivial. For when any state of affairs *A* passes into another state of affairs *B*, either it does so in accordance with the laws of nature or it does not, and in the latter case we have a miracle. But no educationist seriously maintains that the changes which form a child's growth are miraculous. If, indeed, they are then there is certainly no point in studying education. Hence our proposition, interpreted in this sense, says nothing about the child which is not obviously true.

What then did those educationists mean who put forward this proposition? What they meant was, I think, something like this. To describe the changes which take place in any system (whether the system be a physical, chemical, biological, or psychological one), we need to know two sets of things. We need to know first of all the initial state of the system, and secondly, we need to know the natural laws involved. For example, to describe the changes which take place when a stone is let fall from the top of a cliff, we need to know the initial conditions of

---

1 Such a proposition has been held to be true by Rousseau, Pestalozzi, Froebel, for example.

projection and the law or laws governing the motion. Similarly, to describe the changes which take place when a plant grows, we need to know the kind of seed which was initially planted, and secondly, the laws which govern the interaction between that kind of seed and the environment (temperature, humidity, constitution of soil, etc.). Hence to describe the changes which take place during the growth of a child we need to know the initial (that is, hereditary) state of the child, and the laws which govern the interaction between that state and the environment. So far I think most people would agree. But those educationists who put forward the proposition which we are considering maintain something more. They maintain that the initial state of the child and the laws which govern the interaction between that state and the environment are analogous to the seed of a plant and the laws which govern the interaction between that seed and the environment. It is this further claim which justifies these educationists saying that they advocate 'Education according to Nature'. They regard the process of education as analogous to (in the sense described) certain *natural* processes, where 'natural' is now used in the sense in which it is opposed to 'artificial'. Or, to put it in another way, they regard the process of education as analogous to certain processes which occur in the *World of Nature*. The teacher should thus act like a gardener who affords a plant every opportunity for 'natural' growth, and should not act like a gardener who attempts to do something 'unnatural' with a plant.

The crucial question for such a view of education is how far does this analogy hold? There is no doubt that there is some analogy between the laws governing the physical development of the child and the laws governing the development of a plant, and hence there is some justification for the view if applied to physical education. But the educationists who hold this view are not generally very much concerned with physical education, and the view is certainly false if applied to mental education.[1] For some of the laws that govern the mental changes which take place in a child are the laws of learning. Now although psychologists are not all agreed about the correct explanation of the various laws of learning, there is general agreement that there are three main types of learning:[2] (a) the process of 'conditioning', (b) learning by trial and error, and (c) learning by what the Gestalt psychologists have called 'Insight'. But the laws[3] which have been found to hold for these three processes have no analogy at all with the laws which govern the interaction between a seed and its environment. Hence our original proposition, 'a child's education ought to be such that it is free to develop according to the laws of its own nature', if interpreted in this way, is false; and therefore there is no justification for the view that a child should be educated 'according to Nature' with this interpretation of such a phrase.

[1] I use this term to include what is generally called intellectual and moral education.
[2] Although some psychologists hold that these three types are not independent. [3] See below, pp. 96–104.

The second proposition which I wish to consider is concerned with intellectual education. 'Sense impression of Nature is the only true foundation of human instruction; because it is the only true foundation of human knowledge.'[1] Some educationists have not been content to rest here, but have gone further and held that, for example, 'all things essentially related to each other should be brought to that connexion in the mind which they really have in Nature'.[2] This extension seems certainly to be a mistake. Edinburgh is related to London in the world of nature by the relation 'north of'. But it is clearly absurd to say that in my mind the idea of Edinburgh should be north of the idea of London. Nor is it correct to take the more charitable interpretation and say that the ideas of London and Edinburgh ought to cause in my mind the idea of the relation 'north of'. For there is clearly no reason at all why I should not think of London and Edinburgh without thinking of their geographical position. Hence I shall consider only the original proposition which maintains that the only foundation of intellectual education is sense impression of nature, and that in this sense a child ought to be educated 'according to Nature'.

Let us consider first of all the reason given for this view, namely, sense impression of nature is the only true foundation of human knowledge. In what sense is this true? It seems to me that there is an important sense in which it is

1 J. H. Pestalozzi, *The Method*. Froebel and Montessori also hold such a view.   2 Op. cit.

true, but so far as I know none of the educationists who hold this view have stated what that sense is. Suppose I look at a table in this room and say 'this table is brown'. Then it is true that my sense impression is the foundation of my knowledge that this table is brown. It is the foundation of my knowledge in the sense that it is logically impossible for me to judge 'this table is brown' unless I am actually having a sense impression of the table. Consider, however, the proposition, 'The Prime Minister of Great Britain lives in Downing Street'. It is certainly as true that I have knowledge of this proposition as that I have knowledge of the proposition 'this table is brown'. But what sense impression is the foundation of my knowledge in this case? It is clear, I think, that in this case there is no sense impression which corresponds to my knowledge as my sense impression of the table corresponded to my knowledge in the previous case. Consequently our knowledge appears to be in this position. There are certain propositions, for example, 'this table is brown', knowledge of which is logically dependent on corresponding sense impressions, and there are other propositions, for example, 'The Prime Minister of Great Britain lives in Downing Street', knowledge of which does not seem to depend on corresponding sense impressions.

But although knowledge of the proposition, 'The Prime Minister of Great Britain lives in Downing Street', does not depend on a corresponding sense impression, it does depend on some sense impression. The easiest way of seeing this is, I think, to realize the distinction between what Mr Bertrand Russell calls 'knowledge by acquaintance' and 'knowledge by description'. 'I say that I am *acquainted* with an object when I have a direct cognitive relation to that object, that is, when I am directly aware of the object itself.'[1] According to Russell there are at least two sorts of objects of which we are directly aware, namely, particulars and universals. 'An object is known by description when we know that it is the so and so, that is, when we know that there is one object, and no more, having a certain property.'[2] Knowledge of an object by acquaintance depends, therefore, on a corresponding sense impression. But it is possible to know a thing by description, in which case we have knowledge of certain characteristics and have knowledge that these characteristics belong to the thing. Indeed, it is clear that most of our knowledge is knowledge by description.

Russell, however, argues that knowledge by description is dependent on sense impression, although to knowledge of a given object by description there is no *corresponding* sense impression. 'The fundamental epistemological principle in the analysis of propositions containing descriptions is this: Every proposition which we can understand must be composed wholly of constituents with which we are acquainted.... The chief reason for supposing the principle true is that it seems scarcely possible to believe that we can make a judgment or entertain a supposition without

1 Bertrand Russell, *Mysticism and Logic*, p. 209.
2 Op. cit. pp. 214–15.

7

knowing what it is that we are judging or supposing about.'[1] It therefore follows that if I can understand the proposition, 'The Prime Minister of Great Britain lives in Downing Street', it must contain only constituents with which I am acquainted, that is, constituents of which I am having or have had some sense impression. All that is then necessary for me to understand the proposition is that I should have knowledge by acquaintance of certain characteristics and know that these characteristics belong to one and only one individual. If this is correct it follows that knowledge by description is also founded on sense impression. Hence the proposition, 'sense impression of nature is the only true foundation of human knowledge', is true in this sense explained by Russell.

Does it follow that the original proposition 'sense impression of nature is the only true foundation of human instruction' is also true? It does not seem to me that it does.

(1) We have seen that although sense impression is the foundation of both knowledge by acquaintance and knowledge by description, yet the latter is, in some way, a construction out of sense impression.[2] It is clearly just as important that the nature of this construction should be realized as that the basic sense impressions should be experienced. It is true that oxygen and hydrogen are the foundation of water, but no chemistry teacher would

---

1 Russell, *Mysticism and Logic*, p. 219.
2 The way in which it is a construction out of sense impression is analysed in Russell's *Theory of Descriptions*.

consider that it was unnecessary to say how water was constructed out of oxygen and hydrogen. On the contrary, knowledge of the way in which oxygen and hydrogen combine to form water is quite as important as knowledge of the fact that it is oxygen and hydrogen and not, say, carbon and oxygen that form water.

(2) Both knowledge by acquaintance and knowledge by description are types of knowledge directed towards objects. But a great deal of our knowledge is not knowledge of objects at all, as, for example, our knowledge of the laws of nature. The law that magnetized bodies attract each other is not primarily a statement about existing objects. It states that if any two bodies are magnetized then they will have some other property as well, but whether there are magnetized bodies or not is not stated. It is true that our knowledge of such a law of nature is founded on our sense impressions and is obtained by induction from our knowledge of propositions about objects. But it is not itself a proposition about objects. Now it must be one of the purposes of instruction to ensure that the child does obtain such knowledge, and is able to arrive at such inductive conclusions by itself. If so it follows that sense impression of nature cannot be the *only* true foundation of human instruction.

(3) An equally serious objection is that if the only true foundation of human instruction is to be sense impression of nature, arithmetic and mathematics have no place in the foundation of human instruction. The supporters of this

view of education do not admit such a conclusion, and there exists a great mass of literature ostensibly explaining how arithmetic and mathematics can be taught by means of sense impressions which the child receives from various pieces of apparatus. I do not propose to consider the value of such apparatus in the education of a child, but I think it cannot be too strongly emphasized that the view which imagines that arithmetic and mathematics must or can be taught by means of such apparatus is based on a completely wrong idea as to the nature of these subjects.

Moreover, the different theories [1] concerning the nature of arithmetic and mathematics are in complete agreement as regards the present question and in complete disagreement with the views of those educationists whom we are considering. The latter generally urge that arithmetic should be taught in some such way as the following. The child must first of all learn the 'meaning' of the different number concepts. Thus the meaning of the concept 'two' is taught by showing the child two beads, two spoons, two children, etc. The different addition combinations are then taught by showing the child that two beads when placed beside three give five beads; that two spoons when placed beside three spoons give five spoons, etc. In this way the child also sees that when one bead is placed beside four beads the same result is obtained as when two beads are

[1] The different theories are 'The Logistic Theory' or 'Logicism', 'The Formalist Theory' or 'Formalism', and 'The Finitist Theory' or 'Finitism'. For a possible reconciliation, see R. Carnap, *The Logical Syntax of Language*, pp. 325–8.

placed beside three beads. The arithmetical proposition that $1+4 = 2+3$ is thus proved. Now all this is really irrelevant as far as the teaching of arithmetic is concerned, for arithmetic is not the least bit concerned with what happens when beads are placed together. This will be at once admitted if it is considered what would happen if no objects such as beads existed and if drops of mercury on a table were used instead. The child could, as before, learn the alleged meanings of 'one', 'two', 'three' and so on, but if one drop were added to four drops the result would sometimes be five drops and sometimes four drops. But whatever the result there would be no temptation to say that the laws of arithmetic had changed; that is, the laws of arithmetic are quite independent of any operations with physical bodies, and may sometimes apply to experiments with these bodies and may sometimes not apply.

How then are we to regard the laws of arithmetic and how should they be taught? I think the answer is that the laws of arithmetic (and indeed of mathematics) should be regarded in the same way as rules of grammar and should be taught accordingly. There are certain symbols in our language generally denoted by marks similar to '1', '2', '3', etc., which are always used in accordance with certain rules, these rules being what are generally called the laws of arithmetic. The rules should and indeed must (if the child is to have any idea at all of what he is doing) be taught in the same way as the grammatical rules of any language are taught.

It may be objected that many people have learned arithmetic by the 'bead method', and the fact that they have got on well in life and have mastered arithmetic perfectly proves that the method is eminently successful. This objection rests on a confusion. If I speak French perfectly it may be said that I have perfect knowledge of the rules of French grammar, yet it is clearly possible that I have never heard of the rules of grammar at all. Similarly, it is possible that people may go through life and through all 'number situations' without making a mistake, and yet it is possible that they have never heard of the grammar of number. It may now be said that if I speak French perfectly then it doesn't matter if I don't know the grammar, and similarly if I never make any numerical mistakes in any situation then it doesn't matter if I don't know the grammar of number, and in a sense this objection is valid. But it should be remembered that for most people some knowledge of French grammar does help them to speak correctly, and that some knowledge of number grammar does help them to count correctly. And it must always be remembered that learning French grammar is not the same as learning French and similarly learning number grammar (arithmetic) is not the same as counting beads, spoons, etc.

Now just as the rules of grammar of a language are independent of the particular meanings of the words in the language, so the laws of arithmetic are independent of the applications of the symbols of arithmetic to the world of physical objects (as we saw from a different point of view in

connexion with the example about the drops of mercury).
Hence the foundation of instruction in arithmetic cannot
be sense impression of physical objects.

To prevent misunderstanding perhaps I should state that
I do not mean that no 'bead instruction' should be given.
On the contrary, in many ways it is more important than
instruction in the grammar of number, just as learning a
language is more important than learning the grammar of
the language. I think instruction should be given both in
arithmetic and in the application of arithmetic; what I have
objected to here is the practice which assumes that there
are only the applications. It is only by keeping clear the
distinction between arithmetic and its applications that we
can hope to combat the nonsense written about the 'real
meaning of numbers', and to instil in the child a clear idea
of what he is doing when he uses arithmetical language.

Thus although I think there is a sense in which it is true
to say that sense impression of nature is the only foundation
of human knowledge, I think it is false to say that it is the
only foundation of human instruction.

The third proposition which I wish to consider is concerned with moral education. 'A child is to be morally
educated by exposing it to the natural consequences of its
own acts.' Perhaps the clearest exposition of the meaning
of this proposition has been given by Herbert Spencer:
'When a child falls or runs its head against the table it
suffers a pain the remembrance of which tends to make it
more careful; and by repetition of such experiences, it is

eventually disciplined into proper guidance of its movements. If it lays hold of the firebars, thrusts its hand into a candle flame or spills boiling water on any part of its skin, the resulting burn or scald is a lesson not easily forgotten. So deep an impression is produced by one or two events of this kind that no persuasion will afterwards induce it thus to disregard the laws of its constitution. Now in these cases Nature illustrates to us, in the simplest way, the true theory and practice of moral discipline.'[1]

Spencer gives three arguments in support of this view:

(1) All theories of morality agree, he says, that conduct whose total results, immediate and remote, produce pleasure is good conduct; while conduct whose total results, immediate and remote, produce pain is bad conduct. Hence we cannot refuse to class bodily conduct as right or wrong according to the pleasure or pain produced by the results.[2]

(2) The penalties which follow in education of this nature are not artificial and unnecessary inflictions of pain, but are unavoidable consequences of the actions which they follow. Further, these painful reactions are proportionate to the transgressions; a slight accident brings a slight pain; a more serious one, a severer pain.

(3) These natural reactions which follow the child's

1 Herbert Spencer, Essay on *Moral Education*.
2 Spencer's actual words are 'all theories of morality agree that conduct whose total results are beneficial is good conduct'. 'Beneficial' is extremely ambiguous, and I think it is clear from the context that his meaning is what I have stated.

wrong actions are constant, direct, unhesitating and not to be escaped; and very soon, recognizing this stern though beneficent discipline, the child becomes extremely careful not to transgress.

Arguments (2) and (3) need not detain us long. It is true that the penalties which follow in education of this nature are unavoidable, are constant, and are not unnecessary inflictions of pain if we assume that the child should be exposed to the consequences of its own acts. But as this is precisely the proposition to be proved the argument is irrelevant. The crux of the question is clearly argument (1). For unless argument (1) is valid, there is no reason for supposing that when the child does act in such a way as to produce results which give pleasure and not pain he is acting rightly.

Let us then consider argument (1) in some detail. The proposition that conduct whose total results produce pleasure is good conduct, and that conduct whose total results produce pain is bad conduct is ambiguous in so far as it is not specified whether pleasant to the individual or pleasant to society as a whole is meant. If it is the former, then the proposition is certainly false, as everyone would agree that bad actions may produce results which give pleasure to the individual who does them. If it is the latter, then I do not see how the argument is relevant to the proposition that a child should be morally educated by exposing it to the consequences of its own acts. For a child is unable to understand any but the most immediate of the consequences of its acts,[1] and even if we assume that it could understand the effects on society as a whole, there is no reason to suppose that it would decide to repeat only those actions which give pleasure to society. Thus if we consider what is meant by 'pleasant' in Spencer's argument it seems to me we must conclude that the argument is either false or irrelevant to the proposition which it is supposed to prove.

But there is also a further weakness. Suppose we admit that 'pleasant' does mean 'pleasant to society as a whole'; and suppose we also admit that a child can determine whether the consequences of its acts give pleasure to society; and suppose still further we admit that a child is always so constituted that it will repeat only those acts which do give pleasure to society and that it will not repeat those acts which do give pain to society. Would it then follow that a child should be morally educated in this way?

I do not think that it does. Spencer says that all theories of morality agree that conduct whose total results, immediate and remote, are pleasant is good conduct, where 'pleasant' is now to be understood to mean 'pleasant to society'. Now I believe that this is true, but all theories of morality have not meant the same when they have agreed. For brevity I shall consider the proposition, 'conduct with pleasant results is good conduct', and by this proposition I mean 'conduct whose total results, immediate and remote,

1 The first age level at which the Stanford-Binet tests test the understanding of the causal relationship is Year VIII.

are pleasant to society as a whole is good conduct'. This proposition, 'conduct with pleasant results is good conduct', has at least three interpretations:

(*a*) Pleasant results are always to be found associated with good conduct.

(*b*) Pleasant results always provide the reason for calling conduct good.

(*c*) Pleasant results are what we mean by good conduct.

The differences between (*a*), (*b*) and (*c*) may be made clearer by the following comparisons. It is true that reflex actions are always to be found associated with a body which is controlled by a mind, but it is not true that the existence of reflex actions provides the reason for saying that a body is controlled by a mind. Again, it is true that certain types of bodily behaviour provide the reason for saying that a body is controlled by a mind, but it is not true that these types of bodily behaviour are what we mean by a body controlled by a mind. Thus propositions (*a*), (*b*) and (*c*) must be carefully distinguished from each other, and theories of morality which agree that 'conduct with pleasant results is good conduct' may mean any of the three.

Now I am not concerned with what theories of morality have actually held (*a*), and what ones have actually held (*b*), and what ones have actually held (*c*). But I think it is important to decide which of these propositions is true. Proposition (*c*) can, I think, be proved false by the familiar type of argument known as the open question.[1] Consider

1 See, for example, G. E. Moore, *Principia Ethica*, chap. 1.

the question, 'is conduct which produces pleasant results good conduct?' This question, even if we assume that the answer is always in the affirmative, is never a tautologous question, that is, it is never equivalent to the question, 'is conduct which produces good results good conduct?' But if proposition (c) is true, then it ought to be a tautologous question. For example, it is true that 'rich' is what we mean by 'wealthy', and the question 'is a wealthy man rich?' is clearly silly in the sense of being tautologous. But the question, 'is conduct which produces pleasant results good conduct?', is never silly in this sense. Hence proposition (c) cannot be true.

Proposition (b) also seems to me to be false, but the only reason I can give is that it does not describe the method by which we do actually decide whether an action is good or bad. There are many instances in which we pronounce an action to be good or bad without considering whether it does or does not produce a balance of pleasure or pain in society as a whole. Those who hold proposition (b) to be true will no doubt say that in these cases we are mistaken, and I do not see any method of proving such people wrong. Nevertheless, I am quite certain that they are wrong.[1]

Proposition (a) is, I think, true; that is, the results of a good action do produce pleasure in society as a whole. But

[1] One reason for my certainty is that it would always be possible to doubt if any action was good or bad by pointing out the possibility of some effects which had hitherto been ignored. But it seems to me there are certain cases where it is not possible to doubt that an action is good or bad.

this is true solely as a matter of fact, and not because of any necessary connexion between goodness and pleasure.

Hence we must come to the conclusion that when Spencer says all theories of morality agree that conduct whose total results immediate and remote produce pleasure is good conduct, what he means, or should mean, is that they agree that pleasure is, as a matter of fact, associated with good conduct. But from that, the conclusion of his first argument does not follow. His conclusion was that we cannot refuse to class bodily conduct as right or wrong according to the pleasure produced by the results. But we have seen that the pleasure produced by the results is not what we mean by good conduct, nor is it the reason for calling conduct good. Thus Spencer's first argument is invalid, and he has therefore failed to provide any satisfactory reason why we should believe that a child is to be morally educated by exposing it to the natural consequences of its own acts.

The fourth proposition which I wish to consider is this: 'The education of the child should be a process which is similar to that through which mankind has passed in the course of its evolution.'[1] It is certainly true that many animals in the course of their growth pass through stages each of which is similar to some stage which has occurred in the evolution of such animals. It is also true that the human embryo passes through stages which seem to correspond

---

[1] This has been maintained by Pestalozzi and Herbert Spencer, for example.

with stages which have occurred in the evolution of the human race. It is possibly true that the child passes through mental and physical stages which correspond to later stages in the course of evolution. Thus Stanley Hall, one of the leading exponents of this view, urges that the child between the years of eight and twelve is passing through a period which corresponds to the pigmoid stage of human evolution; even the development of speech in the child is supposed to recapitulate the way in which language developed among our ancestors. From evidence such as that it is urged that the process of education should run parallel as far as possible to the way in which the race has developed. In practice this means two things: (1) Education at each stage of a child's life should make use of those conceptions which were current at the corresponding stage of the race's evolution. (2) Education should ensure that each child is, as far as possible, placed in the attitude of a discoverer, that is, he should be left to find things out for himself instead of accepting results on the authority of the teacher.

It should be emphasized at the outset that there is no general agreement among specialists that the child does pass through mental and physical stages which correspond to stages in the evolutionary development of the human race. But let us suppose that agreement is eventually obtained. Then it seems to me that there is some justification for (1), but very little for (2). I do not mean by this that educationists should act as if (1) were true, and train the child's mental life by conceptions which prevailed in

20

the remote past as the leaders of certain youth movements do at present, for I think it is extremely probable that authorities will eventually agree that there is no such correspondence as has been alleged. What I am more concerned with, however, is to maintain that even if such correspondence is established there is practically no justification for (2).

Those people who have made discoveries in the history of the race have been in a position very different from the child. The actual discoverer, before his discovery, has a great deal of knowledge, knows exactly what gaps have to be filled in, and arranges his experiment in such a way that, so far as he is aware, the gap will be filled in. That is, he knows what facts to pay attention to and what facts to ignore, he knows what hypotheses are worth considering and what hypotheses are not worth considering, and he knows how to test those hypotheses which are. But the child has none of all this, and it is the function of the teacher to provide it. This function is fulfilled if the teacher provides and arranges the facts and sets the pupil to derive conclusions from them. That is, the teacher should not set the child to do certain experiments and see if he gets the right results. Rather he should provide the child with adequate information and set him to devise the experiments which will enable conclusions to be drawn.

Some of those educationists, however, who consider (2) to be true do so not only because they hold that there is a correspondence between the stages of child development and the stages of human evolution, but also because they hold that authority should have no place in education.[1] The child, they argue, ought not to accept anything because he is told to accept it, but ought only to accept what he has found out for himself. This raises a point of some difficulty. The opinion has gained ground that it is somehow more 'hard-headed' and 'scientific' not to accept anything on authority, and this has made some educationists feel that if children are to be educated on 'scientific' lines then they must be taught to find things out for themselves.

It should be remembered, however, that the actual practice of scientists is very different, for they are continually accepting results as true which are published by fellow-scientists and I think, by consideration of this fact, we can arrive at some criteria which will decide when it is reasonable to accept anything on authority. I think there are two cases[2] in which it is reasonable.

(1) When our authority is in a position to observe facts which we are not in a position to observe, *provided that in addition* (*a*) other authorities who have been in a position to observe the facts agree, and (*b*) the conclusions which our authority states do not conflict with facts which we are able to observe. For example, we accept certain geographical facts on the authority of travellers if they have

1 Spencer, for example, says: 'They [children] should be told as little as possible and led to discover as much as possible.'
2 See C. D. Broad, *The Mind and its Place in Nature*, pp. 482–4, where a similar question is discussed.

been in a position to observe these facts and we have not, and if in addition (a) other travellers who have been in a position to observe these facts agree, and (b) the conclusions which may be drawn from the facts do not conflict with facts which we are able to observe, such as weather conditions.

(2) The second case in which it is reasonable to accept results on authority is when they are stated as conclusions to an argument which we are unable to follow, *provided that in addition* (a) the argument follows from premises which we know to be true, or if we do not know them to be true, we know are accepted by other authorities, and (b) the argument is considered to be valid by other authorities. For example, it is reasonable to accept a statement by Professor Spearman on psychological statistics if it is the conclusion of an argument which we are unable to follow, provided that (a) we know the premises of the argument to be true or, if we do not know them to be true, we know that Professors Burt, Holzinger, Thomson and Thurstone accept them as true, and (b) the argument is considered to be valid by Professors Burt, Holzinger, etc.

Hence I think it is quite clear that far from it being 'unscientific' to accept results on authority, it may be extremely scientific, and it certainly seems to me that education would be quite impossible unless it is done. If that is so, then it follows that there is no ground for the view that the child ought to be placed as far as possible in the attitude of a discoverer and left to find things out for himself.

CHAPTER II

The Educational Theory of Johann Friedrich Herbart

In this chapter I shall attempt to expound a theory of education which has had very great influence, particularly in Germany and in the United States of America. The theory, originally set forth by Herbart (1776–1841), has been modified in various ways by his followers, and in what follows I shall not attempt to distinguish between what is due to Herbart and what is due to these followers. It is the type of theory in question with which we shall be concerned, rather than the literal exposition of it by any individual or set of individuals, but since it is convenient to have a name for it, I shall call it Herbart's, as its main features are undoubtedly due to him.

There are three main divisions of Herbart's theory: (1) his theory of Ethics, which gives the aim that teachers should pursue, (2) his theory of Psychology, (3) his principles of teaching, which apply his psychological theory so as to give the means by which his aim is to be realized. Different writers have laid different emphasis on these three divisions. Some regard the theory of ethics as the most important of the three, and maintain that Herbart's contribution here is of value even if his theory of psychology is false.[1]   Others consider that his theory of ethics depends on his views about psychology and that 'without a knowledge of the latter it is impossible to understand the former'.[2] It seems probable that actually his theories of ethics and psychology affected each other, and we shall therefore not attempt to make any sharp division between them.

To the modern psychologist there is no doubt much that is fantastic in Herbart's psychology. On the other hand, I believe that many parts of it are not as absurd as they are commonly considered to be. The basis of his theory is the view which he holds concerning the human soul. This he considers to be originally a *tabula rasa* in the strictest sense. 'The soul', he says, 'is originally a *tabula rasa* in the most absolute sense without any form of life or presentation, consequently there are in it neither primitive ideas, nor any predisposition to form them.' Thus all human souls are alike originally, and all the individual differences which are evident among human beings are due to (1) the differences that originally exist in the bodies of different individuals, and (2) the differences that exist in the environment. This is often considered to be a *reductio ad absurdum* of the views held by John Locke. Locke held that the mind of man was quite blank at birth, but he allowed that individuals may have different mental powers or potentialities. Thus he compares the mind to a white sheet of paper, or to wax to be moulded or fashioned, but he grants that impressions

1 F. H. Hayward, *The Student's Herbart*, p. 8.
2 A. Darroch, *Herbart, A Criticism*, p. 65.

made on the mind will vary according to the natural strength of retention. 'An impression made on beeswax or lead will not last so long as on brass or steel.'[1] Herbart, however, argues that not only are souls alike in being blank at birth, but that they have also the same potentialities, or, as Locke would say, the same 'natural strengths'. This, at first sight, appears to be absurd. For it is indeed obvious that human-minds acquire many characteristics which vary from individual to individual, and it is reasonable to express this by saying that the child at birth has power to acquire these characteristics, and that such powers vary from child to child. Herbart, I think, does not really deny this. What he maintains is that the power to acquire these mental characteristics is not a mental one, but exists because of the union of what he calls soul and body, and that the mental differences between individuals are really due to differences between their bodies or environments.

It seems possible that this view is correct. Stated in more modern language it is roughly this. There are in our experience two apparently fundamental categories, namely, mind and matter, each of which is present in varying form in every individual. Theoretically it is possible that these two categories are not independent; for example, mind may be reducible to matter (Behaviourism), or matter may be reducible to mind (Idealism), or both may be reducible to some third category (Neutralism). Herbart holds yet another alternative, namely, that mind is reducible to

1 John Locke, *Some Thoughts Concerning Education*, § 176.

matter plus a certain factor (called the soul) which is qualitatively the same in every individual. Perhaps an analogy will make this clearer. The properties of sodium chloride, sodium sulphate, etc., are considerably different, but these substances are (in a sense) reducible to a certain element, sodium, which is qualitatively the same in them all, and to certain other elements which are different in the different substances. Similarly, it may be argued that although there are great mental differences between individuals, yet these characteristics may be reducible to a factor which is the same for all and to certain other characteristics (of the bodies) which are different from individual to individual. Mental characteristics of human beings are thus like chemical properties of salts of the same metal. The analogy, of course, is not perfect, as we know that differences in the environment will produce differences in the mental characteristics of individuals, and to this there is nothing corresponding in chemistry.

How far is this basis of Herbart's psychological views true? At first sight it appears to be quite unverifiable, as there is no method of testing whether there are such entities as souls, all qualitatively the same, which unite with physical bodies to produce new individuals. Nevertheless, I think it is possible to verify it to this extent. It would be true if the following assumptions could be established:

(1) Mental phenomena are not reducible in any sense to merely physical phenomena, that is, all varieties of Behaviourism are false.

(2) The more closely two physical bodies resemble each other, the more closely will the mental characteristics associated with these bodies resemble each other.

(3) The more closely the environments of two individuals resemble each other, the more closely will these two individuals resemble each other.

If (2) and (3) are true, then the causes of individual differences are initial differences in physical bodies and differences in environment, which is what Herbart maintained. If, in addition, (1) is true, it follows that there must be some factor which is qualitatively the same in each individual and which is not material. Recent investigations on identical twins and on children brought up as far as possible in the same environment indicate that (2) and (3) are probably true, and (1) is certainly accepted by some psychologists. This basis of Herbart's psychology is therefore reasonably sound.

If it is sound it follows that mind is what is sometimes called an emergent characteristic, and the variations in this characteristic from individual to individual are due to variations either in the original bodily state or in the environment (or in both). Since variations due to the former cause cannot be controlled, the educationist must concern himself with the latter cause. Hence instruction, which is the method by which the educationist attempts to use the environment to fashion the mind of the child, is all-important in education. 'I confess', Herbart says, 'to have no conception of education without instruction, just as on the other hand I recognize no instruction which does not morally educate.' Thus Herbart has little sympathy with those who would leave education to Nature. Life, he argues, is much too short to allow children to pass through all the failures of the race in the course of its evolution; children should be adjusted to their environment as quickly as possible.

Consideration of what is meant by instruction brings us to the two most characteristic conceptions of Herbart's views, the conceptions of many-sided interest and of apperception, but before we discuss these we must inquire into what he takes the aim of instruction or education to be.

Herbart is extremely clear on this point. The whole problem of education for him lies in the conception of morality. Thus the aim of all education is to form character or to produce good individuals.[1] The value of such a statement, of course, lies in the account that is given of what is meant by a good individual, and Herbart explains this at considerable length.

His views are, up to a certain point, similar to those of Immanuel Kant, who was his predecessor in the Chair of Philosophy at Königsberg. Kant held that the only intrin-

[1] Compare an article, 'Religion and National Life', in *The Times*, 17 Feb. 1940: 'It is a right purpose of national education to produce men and women with healthy bodies and intelligent minds and the immense sums devoted to this purpose are well spent. Yet the highest educational aim is to produce good citizens. The basis of good citizenship is character....'

sically good thing that existed in the world was a good will. Other things which are often admitted to be good, such as knowledge, courage, honour, may actually be evil if the will which uses them is bad. The problem is then to give criteria which will help us to decide when an act of will is good and when it is bad. Kant gives three principles to guide us in this decision, the first two being negative and the third positive. (a) The consequences of an act of will are irrelevant to the rightness or wrongness of the act, except in so far as the thought of the consequences affects the act of will. (b) No act which is done impulsively is right. For example, if I give some money to a beggar merely because the sight of him arouses disgust or pity in me, then I cannot be said to have willed rightly. (c) An act of will is right if it is willed in accordance with a certain type of principle. There are two types of principle in accordance with which we can will, and these two types Kant calls Hypothetical Imperatives and Categorical Imperatives. The following example will, perhaps, make clear the difference between these two types. Suppose I consider the possibility of defrauding His Majesty's Inspectors of Income Tax. Before I do so I may reflect that if everyone were to behave in this way the effect would be to produce sheer chaos in our social system, and if I do not desire that I refuse to cheat these amiable gentlemen. In such a case I have acted on a principle, but the principle is a hypothetical imperative, for its aim is to preserve the existence of some kind of order in society. If, on the other hand, I refuse to defraud His Majesty's Inspectors simply because I ought not to indulge in fraud, then I have acted on a principle which I have accepted on its own merits, and such a principle Kant called a categorical imperative. That is, a hypothetical imperative is a principle which is accepted because of the results to which it leads, and a categorical imperative is a principle which is accepted for itself alone. Kant held that I have acted rightly only when I have acted on a principle which is a categorical imperative.

The reason Kant held this view was as follows. He wished to maintain that the rightness or wrongness of an act did not depend on the peculiarities of the individual who performed it. But if the principle on which I act is a hypothetical imperative, then such a view could not be held. For if an individual was so constituted that he enjoyed sheer chaos then he would not be disposed to accept the principle of refusing to defraud His Majesty's Inspectors for the alleged end of preventing chaos. Thus, Kant argued, if the principles of morality are to be universal (that is, are not to vary with the interests, nationality and desires of the individual), they must be categorical and not hypothetical imperatives.

Herbart accepts all of Kant's views except those concerning categorical imperatives. He agrees that the only intrinsically good thing that exists is a good will, and he also agrees with criteria (a) and (b) which Kant gave. Moreover, he agrees with the first part of criterion (c), that is, he agrees that if I act on a hypothetical imperative then my act of will cannot be said to be right, but he disagrees entirely with the second part.

According to Herbart our moral judgements are similar to our aesthetic judgements, and we can give no reason which will justify either kind of judgement. For example, if I ask a musician about the relation between two chords, he may tell me that they form a discord. If I say I don't believe him, he may play me the chords. Then either I recognize at once that there is a discord, or, if I don't, the musician cannot prove to me that there is one. Similarly, Herbart maintained that we have what may be called intuitive knowledge, or knowledge by insight, of the rightness of our acts of will, and that it is not merely impossible to give a proof justifying these moral judgements, but meaningless to talk about justifying them— just as it is meaningless to talk about justifying our aesthetic judgements. (We either hear the discord, or, if we don't, nothing more can be done about it.)

The great difficulty about such a theory is to explain why people disagree so violently on ethical questions. For it appears that one person might, by insight, know that a certain act was right, and another person might, by insight, know that the same act was wrong, and if there is no method of resolving the disagreement then controversy on moral questions would appear to be a waste of time. But since people evidently do not believe such controversy to be a waste of time it would seem that this theory must be mistaken.

Herbart, however, does attempt to avoid this difficulty, for he maintains that there are certain characteristic marks of all right actions. He does not hold that these marks give a definition of what we mean when we call an action right, but that at least some of them are always found to be present when we do so. In a similar way the characteristic 'having thick lips' is not part of the definition of a negro, but it is, nevertheless, a characteristic always to be found present in negroes. There are five such characteristic marks. The first two can be observed only by the person who wills the right act, but the last three can be observed by other people. The five characteristic marks are:

(1) *Inner Freedom.* By this Herbart means the agreement which may exist between the action which we are willing and the judgement of insight on that action. It has often been argued by critics that this is an unsatisfactory mark of a moral action, for it would apply to an immoral as well as to a moral act.[1] For example, if by insight I judge mistakenly that a certain act of will would be good, and if that act of will then takes place, the characteristic of inner freedom would be present, but the act of will would actually be bad. Such a criticism is valid, but I think Herbart meant this characteristic to be used more in a negative than in a positive way. That is, if the characteristic of inner freedom is lacking, which means that I will something which my insight tells me is wrong, then the act of will is bad.

1 A. Darroch, *Herbart, A Criticism,* p. 72.

(2) *Perfection or Efficiency of Will.* It is possible that an individual may judge by insight that a certain act is good and may will that act, but may not have the necessary force of will to carry out the act. 'Reuben, when he willed to save Joseph, submitted to the discernment (insight), which his brethren refused to do; therefore we must praise the former and blame the latter. Reuben acted in accordance with inner freedom, and yet there rests a stain upon him. He had not the necessary force of will to oppose his brethren openly.'[1] This want of energy of will is called lack of perfection or efficiency of will.

(3) *Benevolence*, (4) *Justice*, (5) *Equity*. These last three have their ordinary everyday meanings, and the five together are generally called Herbart's Five Moral Ideas.

We are now in a position to see why the recognition of these Five Moral Ideas does enable Herbart to avoid the difficulty about disagreement on ethical questions. Suppose *A* has insight that a certain action is right, and *B* has insight that the same action is wrong. Then *A* and *B* together can consider if the action does have the characteristic marks of a right action. If *A* finds that it has some characteristic inconsistent with one of the five, then he may, and certainly he should, change his opinion concerning the rightness of the act, while *B* will be reinforced in his opinion of the wrongness of the act. If *A* continues to insist that his original judgement was correct, then *B* cannot prove him

---

1 *Introduction to the Pedagogy of Herbart*, by C. Ufer, translated by J. C. Zinser, p. 44.

wrong, but he need no longer pay serious attention to him. The whole situation is analogous to the knowledge obtained through sense perception. A may see something in the distance which he judges to be a dog, and B may see the same thing and judge it to be a rabbit. They investigate further and try to find if it has any of the recognized characteristics of a dog or of a rabbit (characteristics which have been found by abstraction from a great many acts of sense perception, just as the Moral Ideas have been found by abstraction from a great many moral acts). If they find that it has a characteristic inconsistent with one of the recognized characteristics of a dog then A should change his opinion, and if he does not do so, then B need no longer pay any serious attention to him.

The aim of education, according to Herbart, must therefore be to give the child knowledge of these Five Moral Ideas so that he will be able to choose the good and reject the evil. The next step in the theory is to link this aim of education to the view that instruction is the one thing needful in education, that is, to link the system of ethics to the view of education which Herbart considers is implied by the psychological nature of the child.

Herbart's argument is roughly this. A good individual is one who habitually wills rightly, the meaning of this having now been clarified in terms of the Five Moral Ideas. Our acts of will are determined by our desires when the objects of the latter appear to be attainable; our desires are determined by our interests, and our interests are determined by instruction. It is clear, however, that not all instruction arouses interest. Interest, Herbart argues, is aroused mainly by two types of situation: (*a*) by the perception of any strong sense stimulus, and (*b*) by the acquisition or experience of an idea which fits in with what we already know. The first type of situation becomes less important as we grow older, and the second type is what Herbart calls apperception; that is, apperception is the process by which new ideas are brought into relation with our previous experience and are thus given significance. Apperception is thus the key to the problem of influencing the child's character by means of instruction.

There is no sharp distinction between perception and apperception. In perception we become aware of external objects, but we may not attach much significance to them. When we do become conscious of their meaning, that is, when we can relate them to what we already know, then apperception rather than perception has taken place; and ideas which fuse with each other in this process are called 'apperception masses'.

Herbart gives a number of useful rules which help the teacher to secure that the pupils will always find some connecting link between the new object or idea and what they already know. These rules are called Herbart's five formal steps; actually there are four, but the first is subdivided into two:

(1) *Clearness*. The aim of this step is to obtain clear and distinct ideas in the children's minds. It may be subdivided

into (a) preparation, and (b) presentation. In (a) the existing ideas of the pupils must be analysed and made as clear as possible, and the aim of the lesson should be formulated in as concrete terms as possible. In (b) the new material is offered to the class. This new material must not be presented whole, but should itself be analysed first by the teacher and presented in small logically connected sections.

(2) *Association.* After the new material has been presented to the pupils, an attempt should be made to associate it with objects already known. Herbart considers that, in general, this is most easily done by urging the pupils to converse and to say what comes into their minds in connexion with the new material. The association, of course, must not be applied aimlessly, but must be carefully directed by the teacher.

(3) *System.* In this step the new material should be seen in its proper relation to the old. The knowledge which has been arrived at in step (2) is usually somewhat disconnected and fragmentary. In step (3) it should become systematized. For example, if the new material is some fact in one of the natural sciences, step (2) may consist in the recall of similar facts and step (3) in the formulation of a natural law to cover all such facts.

(4) *Application.* The knowledge obtained by the previous steps should now be tried out or applied by the children. This step is of vital importance and has been emphasized by almost all writers on education since Herbart. 'When a resolve or a fine glow of feeling is allowed

to evaporate without bearing practical fruit it is worse than a chance lost; it works so as positively to hinder future resolutions and emotions from taking the normal path of discharge....Rousseau, inflaming all the mothers of France, by his eloquence, to follow nature and nurse their babies themselves, while he sends his own children to the foundling hospital, is the classical example of what I mean. But everyone of us in his measure whenever, after glowing for an abstractly formulated good, he practically ignores some actual case,...treads straight on Rousseau's path.'[1]

Numerous examples of lessons, constructed in the way suggested by these five steps, will be found in text-books on Herbart. For us the important point is that Herbart maintained that if instruction was moulded along the lines of these five steps, then what he called a many-sided interest would be aroused in the pupil. This conception of many-sided interest is discussed at great length by Herbart, but again for us the main point is that many-sided interest is a well-balanced general intellectual activity which should be caused by instruction. 'He who has a firm grasp of his knowledge,' says Herbart, 'and seeks to extend it, is interested in it.' It is the second clause, the seeking to extend knowledge, that is the essence of interest. Hence it is not true to say that Herbart's view at this point is merely the same as the view of those teachers who profess to arouse their pupils' interest in their subject. For the latter do so only to secure that the pupils attain knowledge of their

1 W. James, *Psychology*, pp. 147–8.

subject. But for Herbart a well-balanced or many-sided interest is the first stage in the realization of the aim of education. For it is the cause of the desires and hence of the acts of will which determine an individual's character. Thus interest is not a means to the end of securing knowledge of the different school subjects, but the different school subjects are means to the end of securing interest.

Herbart's theory may therefore be summed up in the following propositions:

(1) The aim of education is to produce good individuals.

(2) A good individual is one who generally wills rightly.

(3) A right volition has five characteristic marks.

(4) The mind of a child is completely blank at birth, and therefore the only method of education is instruction.

(5) Knowledge, the result of instruction, incites volition (that is, affects character) only when it is connected with interest.

(6) Interest is aroused by proper methods of instruction, therefore the teacher must follow certain rules.

There are two major criticisms which are commonly urged against Herbart's type of theory, and to these we must now turn. The first criticism is that the theory gives a false account of mental life. We have seen that Herbart believed that the mind of a child grew from literally nothing by means of the ideas presented by the teacher in 'apperception masses'; and he gives a long account of how these ideas fuse with or repel further ideas. In short, it is urged that the mind, for Herbart, is simply a collection of apperception masses, the collection being formed by certain principles governing the interaction of these masses. But this criticism goes on to point out that each mind is conscious of itself, that is, 'there must be some one apperception mass which is appercipient to every other apperceived mass'.[1] In other words, if the mind is a collection of groups of ideas, then one of these groups must be the idea of the self, and that group must therefore be aware of every other group. The criticism in question holds that this is absurd.

This criticism I do not believe to be valid. Let us consider an analogous case. It is true that a nation preserves a continuity through successive generations of the individuals who compose it. On the other hand, there is a sense in which it is true to say that a nation is nothing apart from the individuals who compose it. A nation preserves a continuity in that some statements, for example, 'England and Wales are united', about it are true, while the same statements about any set of individuals, living or dead, would be false or even nonsense. But a nation is nothing apart from the individuals who compose it in the sense that any sentence which is about the nation in question can always be translated into a sentence (or sentences) about the individuals who compose it or have composed it. Thus 'England and Wales are united' can always be translated

[1] A. Darroch, *Herbart, A Criticism*, p. 14.

without loss of meaning into sentences which are about individuals. Or, to put it in another way, if we said everything that could be said about several million living and dead individuals then we would have said what is stated by the sentence, 'England and Wales are united'.

Similarly, an individual's mind preserves a continuity through all the apperception masses which compose it, but there is, nevertheless, a sense in which it is true to say that the mind is nothing apart from the masses which compose it. It is true in the sense that if we were to say all that could be said about the apperception masses then we would have said all that could be said about the individual's mind. In more technical language we can say that the mind is a *logical construction*[1] out of apperception masses, and that a nation is a logical construction out of the individuals who are ordinarily said to compose it. It is perhaps misleading to say that the mind consists merely of apperception masses, just as it is misleading to say that a nation consists merely of the individuals who have composed it and who now compose it. Rather we should say that we have two ways of talking about the same set of facts. We can talk about the things which Englishmen and Welshmen have done and are doing, or we can talk, on some occasions at any rate, about England and Wales. Similarly, we can talk about apperception masses or about the mind. Thus although 'England' is never equivalent to a set of Englishmen, and the mind is never equivalent to an apperception mass, yet

1 J. Wisdom, 'Logical Constructions', *Mind*, 1931–2.

it is possible to say everything we need to say using only 'Englishmen' and 'apperception masses'.

Now Herbart attempts to say all that can be said about apperception masses, and therefore it is not a valid criticism of him to say that it is necessarily an incomplete account of mental life. It is true that the details of his actual account appear sometimes to be extremely far-fetched, but his *type* of theory is not thereby proved to be either false or in-adequate. Moreover, from the point of view of the teacher the emphasis laid on apperception has been very valuable as it has led to the practical teaching rules formulated above.

The second major criticism of Herbart's theory is that it is a completely deterministic one and that any deterministic theory of education is false. It will be readily admitted, I think, that Herbart's theory is deterministic, and it therefore remains for us to consider the question, which is often raised even to-day, as to whether any deterministic theory of education must be false.

The arguments against such a theory are of two kinds. There are first of all the arguments which are commonly urged against Determinism in the mental sphere, and there is, secondly, an argument specifically connected with education. The latter is easier to deal with, so we shall take it first. It is sometimes put in the form of a dilemma. If Determinism is true, then education is useless. For if the condition of the universe determines that an individual, when confronted with the choice of either A or B, will choose A and reject B, then whether he is educated or not will make no difference. Similarly, if it is determined that he will choose B and reject A, education is equally useless. Thus we must choose between the truth of Determinism and the usefulness of education. If education is of any use, that is, if education does have power to influence the acts of will of an individual, then Determinism is false, and if Determinism is true, then education is useless. Since, however, all educationists at any rate agree that education is of use, then Determinism must be false, and in particular a deterministic theory of education must be false.

The weakness of this argument is very apparent. Determinism does not imply that an individual, when confronted with the choice of either A or B, will choose A and reject B (or vice versa), independently of all other circumstances. It is generally agreed that physical laws, at least on a macroscopic scale, are deterministic and that, for example, water will flow downhill. But if a particular sample of water is kept under conditions such that it is not allowed to flow downhill, then the law does not have a chance to operate. Similarly, there may be a law to the effect that a human mind under certain conditions will make a certain choice, but if the conditions are altered then that particular law will not have a chance to operate. Now it is precisely this that education has to achieve, that is, education has to alter the conditions to such an extent that when each individual is confronted with a choice then he will choose that alternative which is considered best. Thus this objection to the educational determinist is invalid.

On the other hand, I think there is a great danger that the determinist, as teacher, may become what is popularly called fatalistic. Sir Arthur Eddington has expressed this danger in another connexion with his customary clarity. 'What significance is there in my mental struggle to-night whether I shall or shall not give up smoking, if the laws which govern the matter of the physical universe already pre-ordain for the morrow a configuration of matter consisting of pipe, tobacco, and smoke connected with my lips?'[1] Similarly, the determinist teacher may sometimes question the significance of his efforts, if the laws of the universe already pre-ordain that these efforts are doomed to failure. The answer to this, as we have seen, is just that the laws of the universe pre-ordain no such thing unless the teacher abandons his efforts. Determinism does not imply that the future is determined independently of what an individual does, rather it implies that the future is determined by what he does. Thus the importance of the teacher is enhanced and is not diminished by the acceptance of Determinism.

The general arguments against Determinism in the mental sphere are themselves of two kinds. The first is based on our alleged intuition of freedom. It is undoubtedly true that when we are confronted with a choice of alternatives A and B, no matter how strongly we desire A we also feel that we always *can* choose B. The determinist may reply that this feeling of freedom is illusory and that in fact no

[1] *Philosophy*, Jan. 1933, p. 41.

choice is open to us, but such a reply seems unconvincing. The argument itself, however, rests on the assumption that there is a 'self' different from the desires, which are represented to be in some sense in control of it, so that when desire for *A* wins the day we have to imagine the self dragged along, perhaps protesting feebly. But the self is actually the desiring self, and when we say that we always could have chosen *B* rather than *A*, we mean (or ought to mean) that it is logically possible that our desires might have been different from what in fact they are. Thus Herbart's contention that our acts of will are determined by our desires when the latter are capable of realization is not in conflict with the feeling that each of us possesses a 'self' which is free, with a suitable interpretation of such a phrase.

The second kind of argument against Determinism is that such conceptions as praise, blame, remorse, etc., have no meaning if Determinism is true, and since they undoubtedly do have meaning, then Determinism is not true. It is argued that if an individual's acts of will are determined by his desires, which in turn are determined by his education in some such way as Herbart suggests, then it is absurd either to praise or to blame him for any action. It would be as reasonable to blame water for flowing downhill. This argument as it stands is quite invalid. For it is known that praise and blame are excellent methods of changing desires and will therefore be useful tools for the determinist to employ as teacher. Most people are perfectly willing to admit that the behaviour of animals is determined, yet praise and blame (including physical punishment) are found very useful in educating them. Thus there is every reason for continuing to use praise and blame even if Determinism is true.

A more serious difficulty arises, however, when we consider remorse. Individuals do suffer from remorse, and it may at first sight appear absurd that this should be so, if they are not free to choose between alternatives. But if we consider what it is that causes the feeling of remorse, I think the difficulty will disappear. For what causes remorse in an individual is the thought that he should have been so bad as to have his acts of will governed by such and such desires. That is, he wishes that his desires could have been changed so that he would have acted differently, he does not wish that he could have acted differently while he retained the old desires. Thus the fact that people do sometimes suffer from remorse supports Determinism rather than refutes it.

There are many other arguments which have been used against a deterministic theory of education, but as far as I can see there are none which cannot be met in some such way as those which we have just considered. It seems to me to be important that educationists should hold a deterministic theory of some kind, not only because of its truth, but also because of the tendency at the present time which leads some educationists to urge that teachers should be much less active than Herbart advocated. They urge that 'spontaneous activity' should be encouraged in the child so that he may express his individuality. By this they appear to mean that the child should do things which are caused directly by his 'inner nature', rather than that desires should be aroused in him which would then lead him to do things. But we have seen that we cannot separate the self from the desiring self, and it is therefore of the utmost importance that the teacher should secure the proper desires in each child.

Herbart at least attempted to work out a theory on such lines. We shall see in Chapter IV that the whole problem must now be tackled in a somewhat different way in view of our knowledge of heredity, of the laws of learning, and so on. But when we consider the amount of biological and psychological knowledge that existed during Herbart's lifetime, we can do nothing but admire the logical nature of his theory and ignore the strange and somewhat fanciful details.

CHAPTER III

The Educational Theory of John Dewey

There is little doubt that the writings of Dewey have had more influence on educational theory than those of any other living thinker. Nevertheless, they are often obscure and are sometimes inconsistent with each other. It is, therefore, difficult to give a clear and coherent exposition of what his educational theory is, and while it is easy to criticize many of his actual statements it is often difficult to be sure that it is not just the statement but also the theory which is at fault.

The philosophic basis of Dewey's theory is what has been called 'Pragmatism' by philosophers. This doctrine, which has been advocated by such eminent men as William James and F. C. S. Schiller, has had much greater popularity in America than in Europe. It is a doctrine concerning the nature of our knowledge. 'If ideas, meanings, conceptions, notions, theories, systems are instrumental to an active reorganization of the given environment, to a removal of some specific trouble and perplexity, then the test of their validity and value lies in accomplishing this work. If they succeed in their office, they are reliable, sound, valid, good, true. If they fail to clear up confusion, to eliminate defects, if they increase confusion, uncertainty and evil when they are acted upon, then they are false.... The hypothesis that works is the *true* one; and *truth* is an abstract noun applied to the collection of cases, actual, foreseen and devised, that receive confirmation in their works and consequences.'[1]

Pragmatism was conclusively refuted by Professor G. E. Moore as far back as 1908,[2] and I shall discuss it very briefly lest the philosophic reader should consider me sadistic in flogging what is undoubtedly a dead horse. On the other hand, many writers on education seem to be quite unaware of the arguments against it.

Moore distinguishes four propositions, all of which Pragmatists wish to assert, and which are implicit in the above quotation from Dewey. These propositions are:

(1) We can verify all those of our ideas which are true.

(2) All those among our ideas, which we can verify, are true.

(3) All our true ideas are useful.

(4) All those of our ideas which are useful are true.

The only proposition of these four which Moore accepts is (2), and for the arguments against the other three, the reader should refer to Moore's paper. Moore's arguments appear to me to be quite irrefutable, and it may well be asked, does not Pragmatism state something else apart from these four propositions? It is difficult to say, as those writers who profess Pragmatism rarely state the theory any more clearly than Dewey does in the above quotation.

1 J. Dewey, *Reconstruction in Philosophy*, pp. 156–7.
2 G. E. Moore, 'Professor James's Pragmatism', *Proceedings of the Aristotelian Society*, 1907–8.

Nevertheless, I believe that most Pragmatists subscribe to the view which William James expressed in the words 'our truths are man-made products',[1] and there does seem to me to be a sense in which this is both true and important.

Hobbes once wrote, 'True and False are attributes of Speech not of things, and where Speech is not, there is neither Truth nor Falsehood.' This asserts, what is certainly the case, that truth is bound up with language. If language did not exist, then the characteristic denoted by 'true' (not merely the word 'true') would not exist; and since language is a man-made product, it follows that in some sense truth is a man-made product. Let us try, therefore, to become clearer as to how truth is bound up with language. Language is used by man for a number of purposes of which the following are perhaps the most important:[2]

(1) To communicate information.

(2) To arouse feelings (as in propaganda and some types of poetry).

(3) To direct people and animals (as in commands).

(4) To express feelings (as in some types of poetry and exclamations).

Now the only use of language with which truth is connected is the first, and the essential unit involved in that use is the proposition. This is what has led many philosophers to assert that it is only propositions which can be true or

[1] Moore discusses this point in the paper mentioned, but the discussion does not seem to me to be as good as the rest of the paper.

[2] Compare C. K. Ogden and I. A. Richards, *The Meaning of Meaning*, pp. 224–7.

false. Other units of language such as questions, commands, etc., are not related to truth or falsity. Language in this first use consists of a set of symbols (vocabulary), and a set of rules. The rules are of two kinds:[1] (*a*) formation rules, or rules which explain how propositions are to be formed from the vocabulary; and (*b*) transformation rules, or rules which explain how propositions can be transformed. Typical of the first kind of rule are grammatical rules, and typical of the second kind of rule are the laws of inference which allow us to pass from one proposition to another. Both kinds of rule are arbitrary, as is also the vocabulary. This has long been recognized as regards grammatical rules, but it is only since the development of 'alternative logics' that it has also been recognized as regards the laws of inference. But if these rules are arbitrary then it follows that to that extent the truth of a proposition is man-made; and this seems to me to be a sense, and a very important sense, in which the Pragmatist statement is true.

But this is certainly not the sense in which the majority of Pragmatists maintain it to be true. Nor do they maintain it to be true in the trivial sense that when an individual alters something in the world, then a proposition which was false before now becomes true. Rather they maintain that when an individual discovers in his own experience that a certain proposition is true, then that individual has made the proposition true. 'Only that which has been organized into our disposition so as to enable us to adapt

1 R. Carnap, *The Logical Syntax of Language*, p. 2.

the environment to our needs and to adapt our aims and desires to the situation in which we live is really knowledge.'[1] This naturally has important educational consequences. 'Thoughts just as thoughts are incomplete. At best they are tentative; they are suggestions, indications. They are standpoints and methods for dealing with situations of experience. Till they are applied in these situations they lack full point and reality. Only application tests them, and only testing confers full meaning and a sense of their reality.'[2] It is clear that this is merely a reformulation of one of the propositions which Moore demolished—we can verify all those of our ideas which are true—together with the implication that it is our verification that makes them true, which is just nonsense. I think it must therefore be granted that the system commonly known as Pragmatism is false in any of its ordinary interpretations and, consequently, that it cannot be used as an argument in support of any educational theory. We have seen that one of the propositions generally held to be implied by Pragmatism—our truths are man-made products—is true, but the sense in which it is true points to a method in education radically opposed to Dewey's. For it indicates, and Dewey denies, that stress should be laid on what are traditionally called the formal subjects—grammar and logic—as it is only in so far as we use grammatical and logical rules that we can be said to make a proposition true.

1 J. Dewey, *Democracy and Education*, p. 400.
2 Op. cit. p. 189.

Dewey's acceptance of the doctrine of Pragmatism has influenced his theory of education, particularly with regard to the aim of education. It does not seem to me that he has held the same view about the aim of education throughout his life, and of course there is no reason why he should. I shall, however, state what I take to be his earlier view as well as what I take to be his later view. I shall do this partly because I am not quite certain that he has actually held the two views, and if I state them both then there is a good chance that he has actually held one of the views, and partly because the earlier view has had great influence among Dewey's followers.

The earlier view Dewey has expressed in this way. 'The radical error which child study would inhibit is, in my judgment, the habit of treating the child from the standpoint of the teacher or parent; that is, considering the child as something to be educated, developed, instructed or amused.... The fundamental principle is that the child is always a being with activities of his own which are present and urgent and do not require to be "induced", "drawn out", "developed" etc., that the work of the educator, whether parent or teacher, consists solely in ascertaining, and in connecting with, these activities, furnishing them appropriate opportunities and conditions.'[1] Thus the child must not be regarded as a 'little man', and school life must not be regarded as a training or preparation for later life. But Dewey did hold that when these conditions were

1 J. Dewey, *Transactions of the Illinois Society for Child Study*, 1895.

satisfied in school life then children would be better suited to take part in adult social life. It is important to note that this result, successful participation in social life, was not put forward as an aim of education, but was held to be a consequence of the successful realization of the aim. Dewey has two arguments in favour of this view of education.

The first is as follows. Any society is a group of people who have approximately the same interests and who work for approximately the same aims. But these characteristics do not apply to the traditional school where there is no spontaneous common activity. Therefore the traditional school is not a natural unit of society. To make a school such a natural unit it is necessary to consider what are the natural interests and activities of the child and to organize the school with the satisfaction of these as an aim. Hence there must be radical differences from the traditional school, and these differences are not merely differences in the type of subject studied but differences in attitude. 'We must conceive of work in wood and metal, of weaving, sewing and cooking as methods of living and learning, not as distinct studies. We must conceive of them in their social significance, as types of the processes by which society keeps itself going, as agencies for bringing home to the child some of the primal necessities of community life, and as ways in which these needs have been met by the growing insight and ingenuity of man; in short as instrumentalities through which the school itself shall be made a genuine form of active community life, instead of a place set apart in which to learn lessons.'[1]

This argument does not justify Dewey's conclusions. It may be admitted that the traditional school is not a natural unit of society, but many educationists have held that the school ought not to be such a unit. It is at least logically possible that an extremely artificial schooling might be the best preparation for participation in social life later. Further I think it is probably because there was not a clear connexion between Dewey's aim and the effect of the realization of that aim on social life that Dewey did hold that aim and did not hold some social aim of education (although he did hold that, as a matter of fact, certain social consequences would follow from his aim).

The other argument in favour of this view of education is that it is consistent with the doctrine of Pragmatism. 'No such thing as imposition of truth from without, as insertion of truth from without, is possible. All depends on the activity which the mind itself undergoes in responding to what is presented from without.'[2] This is merely the same argument as was criticized at the beginning of the chapter. If an idea is useful to a child then it is true, and unless it is useful it is not true.

Although neither of these arguments affords any justification for this view of education it is, nevertheless, possible that the view should be accepted. It has been

1 J. Dewey, *The School and Society*, p. 11.
2 J. Dewey, *The Child and the Curriculum*.

widely accepted and developed by some of Dewey's disciples. A school organized on traditional lines teaches a number of subjects—Mathematics, Languages, History, etc.—and its immediate aim is to secure that its pupils attain efficiency in these subjects, although some other aim may also be, and in general is, held (such as the development of character). Some theory is then necessary to explain, in some such way as Herbart does, why knowledge of these subjects, if it is attained, does lead to the achievement of this further aim. It is true that such a theory is very often taken for granted, and the success of a school is judged by the extent to which it achieves its immediate aim. Now a school organized in accordance with Dewey's aim does not teach a number of subjects. Kilpatrick, perhaps the most famous of Dewey's followers, states that the guiding principle in the organization is the bettering of the present life of the child.[1] In order that this may be secured the following four rules[2] should be observed:

(1) The pupils must propose what they actually do.

(2) They should be allowed to do only those things which will build up certain attitudes.

(3) All learning should be done only if it is necessary for what the pupils have actually proposed.

(4) What the pupils are allowed to do should be guided so as to enrich 'the subsequent stream of experience'.

[1] Introduction to *An Experiment with a Project Curriculum*, by Ellsworth Collings, p. xvii.
[2] Op. cit. p. xvi.

These are the bases of what is now generally called the project method of teaching. The children in consultation with the teacher propose some project. The teacher has power to veto any proposal, and selects the project which is most in accordance with rules 2 and 4. Other considerations also come in. The project must, for example, be practicable; that is, it must not involve apparatus impossible to make or to secure. The project must also be suitable to the age of the children and so on. The pupils then discuss plans for carrying out the project, and it is here that the teacher is probably of most help. The plans are then carried out and a report written which is criticized by the pupils and teachers.

Such a method of teaching must be carefully distinguished from the method often employed in traditional schools, namely, the method of utilizing the child's interests for teaching the various subjects. In the project method, the child's interests and purposes are the important thing, and the various subjects are regarded merely as means for satisfying these interests and purposes.

One minor criticism can be disposed of at once. It is clear that if the school is organized in accordance with these four rules, it is not true to say with Kilpatrick that the guiding principle is the bettering of the present life of the pupils. For both rules 2 and 4 involve reference to the future. It seems, therefore, that it would be better to give rules 1–4 as the principles guiding the organization (since these are the ones actually used), rather than some one general statement. Moreover, these are more consistent with Dewey's own position. 'It will do harm if child study leave in the popular mind the impression that a child of a given age has a positive equipment of purposes and interests to be cultivated just as they stand.... To take the pheno-mena presented at a given age as in any way self-explanatory or self-contained is inevitably to result in indulgence and spoiling.'[1]

But there are several serious criticisms which have been advanced against the project method. The first is that it is possible for the children not to acquire certain types of knowledge if they do not propose projects which are dependent on such knowledge.[2] I think it is true that most of us are aware that a considerable part of our knowledge would not have been acquired if we had been taught by the project method. The project teacher may say that such knowledge must be valueless and that instead we should have obtained valuable knowledge, but I think a sufficient answer to that is just that it is false.

A second criticism is that one of the well-known laws of learning is violated. It is generally agreed that if any skill is to be retained for any length of time, then considerably more practice in it must be given than is necessary for it just to be recalled. It is for this reason that so much drill is given in the traditional type of school for learning such things as the multiplication tables. But if all learning is to

1 J. Dewey, *The Child and the Curriculum.*
2 G. H. Thomson, *A Modern Philosophy of Education*, p. 94.

be done only in so far as it is necessary for what the child has proposed then there is no reason for giving drill. For example, if a child is engaged in a problem which requires the solution of a quadratic equation then he will be satisfied when he has been shown how to obtain the solution. But it is absurd to imagine that he could then solve another problem which depended on the solution of a quadratic equation. Surely it is better to adopt the customary procedure in text-books and to make the child work fifty or a hundred quadratic equations, after which he will be able to solve any problem of that type.

A third criticism is that the whole method assumes that the child has many interests and desires which it is the business of the educationist to satisfy, or according to the less extreme advocates, to guide. But interests and desires can be acquired as well as knowledge, and it seems almost obvious that many which are acquired in the traditional type of school are more valuable than those 'naturally' occurring in the child. For example, an interest in Greek literature or in differential equations or in medieval history is often acquired, and it is surely the case that an interest in such a subject for its own sake is extremely valuable.

For these reasons it seems to me that the project method and the aim of education out of which the project method was developed must be considered inadequate. Dewey seems to have recognized this, for in his more recent writings he has advocated a somewhat different aim. I find his statement of this extremely difficult to follow and so, as far as possible, I shall let him speak for himself. 'I take it that the fundamental unity of the newer philosophy is found in the idea that there is an intimate and necessary relation between the process of actual experience and education....The problem for progressive education is: What is the place and meaning of subject matter and of organisation within experience?'[1] Continuing, Dewey says we need to know what experience is. 'The belief that all genuine education comes about through experience does not mean that all experiences are genuinely or equally educative. Experience and education cannot be directly equated to each other. For some experiences are mis-educative. Any experience is miseducative that has the effect of arresting or distorting the growth of further experience. An experience may be such as to engender callousness; it may produce lack of sensitivity and of responsiveness. Then the possibilities of having richer experience in the future are restricted. Again a given experience may increase a person's automatic skill in a particular direction and yet tend to land him in a groove or rut; the effect again is to narrow the field of further experience.'[2] The trouble with traditional education, Dewey says, is not that the pupils do not have experiences but that they have the wrong kind of experience. 'Everything depends upon the *quality* of the experience which is had',[3] and the quality of an experience Dewey tells us is

1 J. Dewey, *Experience and Education*, p. 7.
2 Op. cit. p. 13.   3 Op. cit. p. 16.

measured in two ways, first of all by its immediate pleasantness or unpleasantness, and secondly by its effect upon later experiences. 'It is his (the educationist's) business to arrange for the kind of experiences which while they do not repel the student, but rather engage his activities, are, nevertheless, more than immediately enjoyable since they promote having desirable future experiences.'[1]

These statements indicate that Dewey is paying less attention to the immediate experiences and more attention to the future experiences of the pupil than he did in his earlier statements about the aim of education. Nevertheless, they still seem to me unsatisfactory. The key word is the word 'desirable', and as everyone who has read John Stuart Mill knows there are at least two meanings of 'desirable' which it is important to distinguish. For example, the sentence 'Beer is desirable in hot weather' means simply 'Beer is desired in hot weather'. But the sentence 'The abolition of slums is desirable' means 'The abolition of slums ought to be desired'. That is, 'the desirable' may mean 'what is desired' or 'what ought to be desired'. If these meanings are substituted for 'desirable' in Dewey's exposition we get the following two statements:

(1) It is the educationist's business to arrange for the kind of experiences which...are more than immediately enjoyable since they promote future experiences which are desired.

(2) It is the educationist's business to arrange for the

1 Op. cit. pp. 16-17.

kind of experiences which... are more than immediately enjoyable since they promote future experiences which ought to be desired.

Now the second statement might clearly be an account of the aim of a teacher in a traditional type of school, and we must therefore conclude that it is the first statement which expresses what Dewey actually means. But according to this statement the child should have any experiences which will make it easier for him to have the experiences he desires in the future. Such a view would justify the training of children to be gangsters or anything at all. It is, I think, the confusion of the first statement with the second which gives Dewey's theory its apparent plausibility.

This later account of the aim of education is not so pragmatic as the earlier, but it still seems to be the acceptance of Pragmatism which prevents Dewey asserting anything to be the end of the process of education. He is continually preoccupied with the guidance of present experience, and the direction of the guidance is to be settled from day to day according to what is most useful. Indeed, Dewey's theory of education may be regarded as the exact opposite of the Jesuit theory. The latter was preoccupied with the end of education and was not particular about the means to reach the end. Dewey is preoccupied with the means and is not particular what end he reaches.[1]

1 I need hardly warn the reader that this, taken literally, is grossly unfair to both the Jesuits and Dewey.

Perhaps I should also refer to another argument which Dewey gives in support of his type of school against the traditional. He urges that the traditional school is autocratic and that his type of school is democratic, and that democracy is inherently better than autocracy—better in the sense that 'democratic social arrangements promote a better quality of human experience, one which is more widely accessible and enjoyed, than do non-democratic and anti-democratic forms of social life'.[1] The validity of this argument depends, I think, on the assumption that the school can be isolated from the rest of the world. If everything outside the school were to remain exactly as it in fact is, then no doubt a democratic school would be better than an autocratic school. But clearly such an assumption is not true; and it may well be that an autocratic school is necessary to establish a democratic world. It is also doubtful, I think, whether the words 'autocratic' and 'democratic' can be used at all in their ordinary senses with reference to a school.

Dewey's pragmatic views have also influenced his conception of the Laboratory School—the name which he gave to a school which he founded while he was at the University of Chicago. His intention was that this school should have the same relation to the Department of Philosophy, Psychology and Education as a scientific laboratory has to the branch of science associated with it. Now the use of a scientific laboratory is (1) to obtain

1 *Experience and Education*, p. 25.

knowledge of facts and laws hitherto unknown, and (2) to test scientific theories by the invention of crucial experiments. Hence we may say that the purpose of the Laboratory School was (1) to obtain knowledge of facts and laws hitherto unknown to educationists, and (2) to test educational theories by the invention of crucial experiments.

Perhaps I should explain what is meant by a crucial experiment. Suppose a number of facts have been observed. Then it is possible to construct many theories all of which will explain the observed facts, and the problem arises as to which of these theories is to be accepted. The recognized scientific procedure is to attempt to deduce theoretically some consequence for each theory which is not implied by any other theory, and then to investigate experimentally which of these consequences is verified. For example, when the observed facts were the motions of the planets of the solar system, it was found possible to construct both the Newtonian and Einsteinian gravitational theories to explain them. Also from Einstein's theory it followed that light should be deflected as it passed through the sun's gravitational field, while from Newton's theory it did not follow. By experiment, however, it was found that such a consequence did take place, and therefore Einstein's theory superseded Newton's. Such an experiment as verifying the deflexion of light in the sun's gravitational field is called a crucial experiment.

If the records of the Laboratory School are examined, however, it becomes clear that the parallel with a scientific laboratory breaks down. It is certainly possible to obtain knowledge of facts hitherto unknown, and from these it may be possible to obtain by induction knowledge of laws hitherto unknown. But it is quite impossible to test educational theories by means of crucial experiments in a Laboratory School. For most educational theories involve some reference to after-school life. Before such a theory could be either confirmed or refuted it would therefore be necessary for knowledge to be obtained not only about the facts of school life but also about the facts of later life, and about the way in which these are connected with the facts of school life. That is, if an educational theory has reference to what happens in after-school life, then it can be neither confirmed nor refuted by appeal to what happens in school only. Hence the Laboratory School can at best fulfil only the first function of a scientific laboratory. This first function of a scientific laboratory—the discovery of hitherto unknown facts—has nothing to do with the verification of theories, and all educationists, whatever the theories they hold, would agree that there should exist schools in which new facts and laws could be discovered. Thus Dewey's conception of the Laboratory School is valuable in so far as the school is not considered to be a place where educational theories are verified and refuted; and it seems to me probable that Dewey would not have regarded it in this second light if he had not been so obsessed by the idea of verification, which in turn was due to his acceptance of Pragmatism.

CHAPTER IV

The Basis of Any Educational Theory

In the previous chapters we have seen that various different views have been held about the nature of education. Other typical definitions are the following:

'I mean by education that training which is given by suitable habits to the first instincts of virtue in children.' (Plato.)

'In the first place, education aims at producing such a character as will issue in acts tending to promote the happiness of the state; in the second place, it aims at preparing the soul for that right enjoyment of leisure which becomes possible when practical needs have been satisfied.' (Aristotle.)

'By education I mean the influence of the environment upon the individual to produce a permanent change in his habits of behaviour, of thought and of attitude.' (G. H. Thomson.)

'Education consists in developing specific habits, memories, ideas, forms of manual and mental skill, intellectual interests, moral ideals, and a knowledge not merely of facts and conclusions, but also of methods.' (*Spens Report on Secondary Education.*)

All these different definitions, and others which have been given throughout the history of the subject, show a certain measure of agreement, but it is clear there are important differences. Does that mean that one definition is correct and the others wrong? Before we can answer that we must find out how we decide whether a definition is right or wrong. It is, for example, sometimes held that we can define words as we please, so long as we do not depart from our defined meaning. On the other hand, it is sometimes held that it is not words we define but things or concepts, and definitions therefore cannot be arbitrary.

According to Aristotle 'a definition is a phrase signifying a thing's essence. It is rendered in the form either of a phrase in lieu of a term or of a phrase in lieu of another phrase.' The difficulty in such an account is to know what is meant by a thing's essence. The Scholastic Philosophers attempted to explain this with the help of the traditional formula 'per differentiam et genus', but such an explanation could, at best, apply only to substantive terms, and it is obvious that there is no justification for so restricting definition. Words such as 'the', 'not', 'plus', 'imply', must be understood as well as 'Man', 'triangle', 'education'.

Definitions may be divided into two classes according as they are 'biverbal' or 'ostensive'. A biverbal definition is a sentence in which one symbol, or set of symbols, is asserted to signify the same as another set of symbols provided that the second set is already understood. Two types of biverbal definition may be distinguished:

(a) The type of definition (such as 'man is a rational animal') which is commonly said to be *real*. This has caused some confusion, because it seems that in some sense definition must be arbitrary, and yet it seems that this kind of definition does convey information. The solution lies in the realization of the fact that such definitions are a conjunction of two kinds of proposition—the one a proposition of what might be called social history, and the other a proposition expressing a command or volition by the person who asserts it. Thus if I assert the proposition 'the characteristic C is defined by the characteristics C_1, C_2, C_3' or, more briefly, 'C is C_1, C_2, C_3', my assertion is equivalent to the following conjunction: 'On suitable occasions in the past there has been general agreement in applying the word C when the words C_1, C_2, C_3, have been applied, and there has been general agreement in not applying the word C when none or some only of the words C_1, C_2, C_3 have been applied. In the future I intend to apply the word C only when all C_1, C_2, C_3 can be applied, and I intend never to apply the word C when some only of C_1, C_2, C_3 are applied.' The first proposition is the proposition of social history—it tells how the word has been used in the past—and the second proposition expresses the volition (sometimes it may express a command). For example, the definition 'man is a rational animal' is equivalent to the conjunction of the following propositions: 'On suitable occasions in the past there has been general agreement in applying the word "man" when the words "rationality" and "animality" have been applied, and there has been general agreement in not applying the word "man" when neither or only one of the words "rationality", "animality" has been applied. In the future, "man" must be applied only when both "rationality" and "animality" are applied, and must never be applied when neither or one only of the words "rationality", "animality" is applied.'

This gives a solution to the controversy between those who say that definition defines words and hence cannot be true or false, and those who say it defines things or concepts and hence may be true or false. For if a definition of this type is equivalent to the conjunction of a proposition of social history and a command, then if the proposition of social history is false, it will follow that it would make sense to say that the definition was false. Moreover, since the command or volition is a command or volition concerning the use of words, it would also make sense to say the definition gave directions how words were to be used. Thus, for example, the definition 'education is the influence of the environment upon the individual to produce a permanent change in his habits of behaviour, of thought, and of attitude' is equivalent to the conjunction of the two following propositions. 'On suitable occasions in the past, there has been general agreement in applying the word "education" when there has been influence by the environment producing changes in the habits of individuals, and there has been general agreement in not applying the word "education" when there has been no such influence.... In the future "education" must be applied only when there is such an influence and must never be applied when there is not such an influence.' Now the first proposition may be false, and indeed from the different definitions which have been given it is clear that at least it is not strictly true. But the second proposition cannot be true or false, as it expresses a command or volition of the person who made it (in this case Professor Thomson). We can see then that to give a completely satisfactory definition of education we must give all the marks which have been thought characteristic of it, and then agree to use the word 'education' only for a process having those characteristic marks.

Before we proceed with this, let me finish the discussion of definition, for it will be of use later.

(b) The second type of biverbal definition is what has been traditionally called biverbal, that is, such definitions as 'valour' for 'courage', and 'riches' for 'wealth' and so on. This type perhaps brings out most clearly the purpose that all definition has to serve, namely, that the second set of symbols must be already understood. There is an important point here. Any given set of symbols can be defined only in terms of another set of symbols, and hence any given set of symbols must, after a finite number of biverbal definitions, be equivalent to a set of indefinable symbols. Now 'indefinable' in Logic does not mean 'not understood', but rather that which is understood, a point that was first clearly made by Johnson. 'A certain misunderstanding as to what in Logic is meant by the indefinable must here be removed; for it has been frequently supposed that the indefinable means that which is admittedly not understood. But so far from meaning the "not under-stood", the indefinable means that which *is* understood; and philosophy or logic may ultimately adopt a term as indefinable only where, because it is understood, it does not require a further process of definition.... The indefinable does not therefore mean that which is presented as having no understood meaning, but that whose meaning is so directly and universally understood, that it would be mere intellectual dishonesty to ask for further definition.'[1]

The second kind of definition is what has been called 'ostensive', and this kind of definition affords an explana-tion of how we acquire knowledge of the use of symbols which are indefinable by biverbal definition. In ostensive definition we point to an object to explain the given set of symbols. From this it might seem that we could give an ostensive definition of Mr Churchill, for example, but not of 'one'. Such is not the case, however, for ostensive definitions differ according to the kind of pointing that is involved. For example, a different sort of pointing would distinguish the ostensive definition of 'one' from the ostensive definition of 'object', although the same thing might be pointed to in both cases. Nor must we take pointing literally. For example, I might give an ostensive definition of the term 'proposition' as follows: when I say 'it is raining' then I have made a proposition. Or I might give an ostensive definition of 'ill' to a child as follows: when the child is obviously suffering from influenza, I

1 W. E. Johnson, *Logic*, Part i, pp. 105–6.

could say, 'You are feeling ill just now.' These last two examples will illustrate the great objection which has been urged against ostensive definition, namely, that the definiendum (the group of symbols to be defined) is not uniquely defined. Thus in the first example the definition would apply to 'sound' as well as to 'proposition', and in the second example the definition would apply to 'uncomfortable' as well as to 'ill'. This objection is certainly valid, but what it amounts to is really that the word 'definition' should not be used to describe the process. For definition is generally taken to be a process which determines uniquely the use of a word, and these two examples do not determine uniquely the use of 'proposition' or 'ill', and hence are not definitions. Let us consider for a moment if this process which has been called ostensive definition ever could determine the use of a word uniquely, and hence satisfy the requirements of a definition as usually understood. Suppose someone shows me a piece of cloth and says, 'the colour of this cloth is x', then this gives uniquely the use or meaning of x. Contrast this situation with one in which someone shows me a piece of cloth and says, 'this is x'. Clearly x might have the same meaning as in the first situation, or it might mean cloth or a number of other things. Now the difference between the two situations is that in the first I know what sort of thing x stands for, whereas in the second I do not. The word 'colour' already fixes part of the use of x. Thus we can say that ostensive definition is definition as usually understood if only one blank is left to be filled.

Otherwise the ostensive definition of a word gives only one rule for the use of a word and one rule is not enough to fix the use.

Let us return now to the biverbal definition of 'education', and let us find what are the characteristic marks of the process to be called education. If the definitions which have been given are examined, I think it will be found that there are four conceptions which are characteristic: (1) the original nature of man; (2) the production of changes in behaviour as, for example, the formation of habits; (3) the environment; (4) the idea of value. The following biverbal definition could therefore be given:

Education is a process involving the action of the environment on the original nature of man in such a way as to produce valuable changes in behaviour.

If this is correct it follows that when educational theories differ, they must do so in the accounts they give of one or more of these four basic conceptions. The remainder of this chapter will be devoted to such an account.

The original nature of man may be studied from very many different points of view. For example, we may study the chemistry of the elements and compounds found in the human body at birth, or we may study the anatomy and physiology of the human body. But clearly this is not what we are interested in when, as educationists, we study the original nature of man. We find without any detailed investigation that the behaviour of different individuals is extremely similar on some occasions and is extremely different on others, and we want to find and, if possible, to control what causes the behaviour sometimes to be similar and sometimes to be different. That is, what we are interested in is the behaviour of human beings, and what we want to know is how much of that behaviour can be altered or modified by education and how much of that behaviour cannot be altered or modified. The original nature of man, therefore, must not be thought of as the sum total of the characteristics of the newly born child but rather as the sum total of those characteristics of the adult, which are responsible for the unmodifiable types of behaviour. Thus when educationists study the original nature of man they seek to classify human characteristics according as they are responsible for modifiable or unmodifiable types of behaviour. This problem is often confused with the biological problem of investigating what characteristics are hereditary and what characteristics are acquired (that is, not hereditary), but the problems, although, as we shall see, closely connected, should be carefully distinguished.

It is important to realize at the outset that there is no sharp division between the types of behaviour which can be modified and the types of behaviour which cannot be modified. We shall commence by describing types which cannot be modified, and we shall end by describing types which can be modified, but we shall not attempt to draw a line in between. The fact that there is no sharp division should not obscure from us the differences that exist, just as the fact that there exists a continuous range of colour extending through orange from red to yellow does not obscure from us the differences between red and yellow.

The first type of action which cannot be modified is that which is imposed by the general nature of our bodies and the environment. For example, throughout my life my body must remain on, or in close proximity to, the surface of the earth, and no educationist has power to modify such behaviour to the slightest extent.

The second type of action is what may be called physiological action, that is, actions which directly keep us alive, such as the digestion of food, respiration, etc. The mechanism of all such actions is practically perfect at birth in normal human beings, and it is impossible to alter or modify such actions to any extent without endangering the life of the individual. Closely related to physiological action is that part of our behaviour which is called temperamental. Temperament is generally defined as the influence of the endocrine and metabolic processes on the nervous system. This influence is due to the effects produced by chemical substances (hormones) which pass into the blood from the endocrine glands[1] and are carried to the brain, where they act upon the nervous tissue. This kind of behaviour can be modified, but only by drugs such as chloroform and alcohol, and it is unlikely that modification of this nature will ever come under the control of the educationist, although it might do so under conditions similar to those imagined by Aldous Huxley in *Brave New World*.

[1] The most important are the thyroid, pituitary and suprarenal.

The next type of action is that known as reflex action. This type is most easily explained in terms of what is called the structure of the nervous system. This phrase 'the structure of the nervous system' does not mean that the nervous system has a structure in the sense in which a molecule of organic chemistry has a structure. The nervous system of any animal is continually changing, but in these changes it is possible to distinguish relatively stable events from relatively unstable events. The class of relatively stable events is called the structure of the nervous system, and the class of unstable events is often by comparison called the function of the nervous system.

The body of any animal is built up of living cells. Some of these cells form groups each of which is generally called an organ, and there are two kinds of such groups which are important from the present point of view. One kind of organ (organs of this kind are called receptor organs or receptors) is peculiarly sensitive to changes which take place in the external world. For example, the organ called the eye is peculiarly sensitive to changes in the wave-length of light. A second kind of organ (organs of this kind are called effector organs or effectors) brings about those changes in the body of the animal by which it adapts itself to the external world. Typical effectors are muscles and glands. What is called the nervous system of the body is a kind of network of cells which links the effectors of the body with the receptors. The unit of this network of cells is called a neurone. A typical neurone consists of a centre together with two kinds of offshoot. The first kind of offshoot is called a dendron (or dendrite), and generally there are several dendrons belonging to each neurone. The second kind of offshoot is called an axon, and there is always only one axon belonging to each neurone. The dendrons generally break up into a number of fine filaments a short distance from the centre, while the axons consist of a long straight part and a bushy 'tail' of filaments. Neurones are connected by the intertwining of these filaments, the axon filaments of one neurone intertwining with the dendron filaments of the neighbouring neurone. The points at which intertwining takes place are called synapses, and a series of neurones linked in this way from a receptor to an effector is called a nervous arc. Each receptor is thus connected in some way or other with each effector, and theoretically a disturbance in the environment which excited one receptor might stimulate very many, or indeed all, effectors. This has been actually observed in some animals when it was found that any stimulus produced a kind of generalized muscular activity.

In any disturbance of the nervous system there are five essential steps: (a) the stimulus of a receptor, (b) the transmission, by some neurone, of an impulse from the receptor towards the central nervous system, (c) the transmission of the impulse through the central nervous system, (d) the transmission, by some neurone, of the impulse from the central nervous system to an effector, (e) the response of the effector. The chief difficulty is to be clear what this disturbance or nervous impulse is, and much work has been done in recent years about this.[1] In the first place it must not be thought that anything is transmitted from receptor to effector; as far as is known there is no transmission of either matter or energy. If this is realized the apparent paradox of what is called the 'All-or-None Principle' is resolved. It is found that for an impulse to pass, the stimulus must be of a certain minimum strength, but that when the stimulus is above this strength the same impulse passes whatever the strength of the stimulus. It is perhaps similar to the situation in which the electric door-bell of a house is rung. Either the button is not pushed and the bell does not ring, or the button is pushed and the bell rings and rings with the same intensity however hard the button is pushed. Thus all we can say is that the nervous impulse is some change of state, possibly the passage of a chemical change, from receptor to effector. In the second place we can say that it passes in the way described, because it takes a finite time, and if the nerve fibres are cut then there is no response of the effector. There are many difficulties still to be solved, but there seems no reason to doubt that the above account is substantially accurate.

Now among all the possible disturbances of the nervous system there are some which are more complicated than others. The nervous impulse may travel a long route in passing from receptor to effector. This happens always

[1] E. D. Adrian, *The Basis of Sensation*, and *The Mechanism of Nervous Action*.

when, for example, a sensation or an act of will occurs, and in such cases the route passes through the higher centres of the brain. But sometimes the impulse takes a very short route, as when it passes from receptor to effector via the spinal cord without passing near the brain. In what is called reflex action the impulse always takes a short route from receptor to effector, and the route is always the same on different occasions. Clearly the shortest possible route would be when a filament of an ingoing nerve makes a synapse with a filament of an outgoing nerve, and this would provide a strict definition of reflex action. Unfortunately, it seems that such a case probably never occurs, and the result is that the term reflex action is used somewhat vaguely for any case in which the impulse takes a reasonably short *fixed* route. In practice we cannot use such a criterion, as in general we can observe only the behaviour of men and animals, and certain behavioural characteristics are used instead. It has been found that when these characteristics are present then the impulse does travel over a short fixed route, and that when the impulse does travel over a short fixed route then these characteristics are present.

The first of such behavioural characteristics of reflex action is that there is a complete lack of spontaneity, that is, there must be a definite stimulus before the action takes place, and the action takes place only so long as there is a stimulus. For example, if the feet of a dog whose brain has been destroyed are stimulated in a certain way, the legs react in a kind of walking movement. This movement is a reflex action, but it is clearly hopeless to expect such action without the appropriate stimulus. A second characteristic is that the same stimulus always produces the same effect. This should be qualified to a small extent, for if conditions are altered sufficiently, for example, if the supply of oxygen or if blood pressure are significantly different from normal, it may not be true. A third characteristic is that the action is generally very localized, that is, the action appears to be the response of part of the organism to the stimulus. There is no evidence that the whole organism is attempting to adapt itself to any change in the environment. These characteristic marks are generally sufficient to decide in any given case whether the action is reflex or not. Typical reflexes in human beings are shivering, starting (at a sudden noise), the knee jerk, sneezing, etc. All such actions can be modified only to a very small extent, but unlike physiological actions they can sometimes be interfered with without endangering the life of the individual. Their existence, however, plays an important part in the conservation of life, as all reflexes are extremely quick and are continually ready for action.

The next type of action in the scale of behaviour from unmodifiable to modifiable is what some psychologists have called instinctive action. Unfortunately, there is no universal agreement among psychologists as to the use of the term 'instinct', and some use the term to cover all unmodifiable types of behaviour. As we have already seen, however, there are different types of unmodifiable behaviour, and it seems desirable to use the term in a somewhat narrower sense. Such a sense has been given by McDougall. 'An instinct is an inherited or innate psycho-physical disposition which determines its possessor to perceive, and to pay attention to, objects of a certain class, to experience an emotional excitement of a particular quality upon perceiving such an object, and to act in regard to it in a particular manner, or, at least to experience an impulse to such action.'[1] The word 'object' should be understood in the widest possible sense, that is, as including not only material things and organisms but also the various situations in which the organism may find itself. McDougall gives the following list of instincts in man: flight, repulsion, curiosity, pugnacity, self-abasement, self-assertion, and the parental instinct. These are the seven main ones and the following five he considers less important: the reproductive instinct, acquisition, feeding, gregariousness, and construction.

In a typical case of instinctive behaviour (in this sense of instinct) some sense impression excites the animal to behave in a particular manner, or at least to strive to behave in a particular manner, which is the same for all animals belonging to the same species on all such occasions. At the same time there is a unique emotional excitement associated with each different case of instinctive behaviour. (The emotions aroused in man corresponding to the seven primary instincts are fear, disgust, wonder, anger, sub-

[1] W. McDougall, *An Introduction to Social Psychology*, p. 30.

jection, elation, and the tender emotion.) Hence there is a threefold aspect of an instinctive act:

(1) The cognitive—some object or class of objects must be perceived.

(2) The affective—emotion must be aroused with regard to the object or class of objects.

(3) The conative—there must be action or at least a tendency towards action with regard to the object.

Objections to this use of the term 'instinct' have been mainly of two kinds. The first kind of objection has been urged by Watson and the behaviourist school of psychologists. Watson observed a large number of infants during the first few months of life and could discover only three emotions exhibited during that period—fear, anger, and love. Fear was aroused on two types of occasion, by a loud noise or by the removal of whatever supported the child; anger was aroused by interfering with the child's movements; love was aroused by stroking, tickling, turning the child on its stomach, and so on. Watson was convinced that there were no indications of any other emotions. From this it is generally argued that McDougall must be wrong, either in his assertion that there is a one-one correspondence between emotions and instincts, or in his list of instincts. But such a conclusion does not follow, if by 'hereditary' or 'innate' McDougall does not mean 'observable in a newly born child'. For example, it is generally agreed that, in some sense of 'hereditary', intelligence is hereditary, but no observations on a newly born child would enable a psychologist to draw any conclusions about its intelligence. Thus Watson's observations are not necessarily inconsistent with McDougall's views.

The second type of objection is more serious. This objection is briefly that this conception of instinct is as useless as the historical conception of faculty. For example, if I run away in a particular situation, then the argument is that to say I do so because of my flight instinct says no more than that I run away. In other words, just as the faculties were class names for some of the usual ways of behaving, so the instincts merely serve the same purpose. Now this would be a valid objection against McDougall's conception of instinct if all he did was to introduce the names of the various instincts. To return to our previous example, if McDougall observed that when bombs dropped people ran away, and said that they did so because they possessed the instinct of flight, then the whole conception of instinct would be trivial. But actually, as we have seen, McDougall does do much more. For he analyses each instinct into a cognitive, an affective, and a conative part. He also holds that instincts are hereditary, although we are not yet clear in what sense that is so, and that there is continuity between the instincts of the various animal species, so that we can to some extent predict the probable behaviour of human beings in a certain situation from the behaviour of animals in that situation. Hence it cannot be maintained that this use of the term 'instinct' is misleading in the sense in which it was misleading to talk of 'faculties'. There is, no doubt, much that is controversial in McDougall's account, but I think it is quite certain that individuals do exhibit uniformity in their affective and conative reactions to certain types of situation, and that such uniformity is transmitted from parents to children. If that is so, then it is certainly desirable to have a name for such reactions, and 'instinctive' seems as good as any. It may, then, be a matter of dispute among experimental psychologists how many instinctive reactions exist in the different animal species, but it does not seem to me that it can be denied that instincts in this sense do exist.

Instinctive behaviour in man can be modified to a considerable extent, very much more than reflex behaviour. Bearing in mind the three aspects of an instinctive action, I think the following exhaust the possibilities of modification:

(1) Instinctive reactions may be aroused not only by the objects which 'naturally' arouse them, but by ideas of such objects or by ideas of objects associated with them. For example, according to McDougall, there exists in man the instinct of curiosity. Part of the work of the teacher is to modify this in such a way that the pupil will react with this instinct when confronted with ideas of the objects which naturally arouse it. The project method, which, as we have seen, insists that the pupils should always be confronted with actual objects or situations, seems to me to ignore the possibility of modifying instinct in this way.

(2) An object may have an affective reaction attached to it different from the one which is 'naturally' attached to it. Thus a loud noise, such as thunder, may naturally arouse the affective reaction of fear, but it is certainly possible for parents to train their children not to experience fear in such a situation.

(3) An object or situation may have a conative reaction attached to it different from the one which is naturally attached to it. For example, if McDougall is correct, there is an instinct of acquisition in human beings by which children tend to appropriate the objects which please them. But parents and teachers generally succeed in modifying this conative reaction even if the original affective reaction remains.

(4) An object or situation may have both an affective and a conative reaction attached to it different from the ones which are naturally attached to it. This happens, for example, in war time, when many people feel emotions and have tendencies towards action with regard to their fellow-man very different from those which their fellow-man naturally arouses.

(5) More than one instinctive reaction may be aroused by the same object. For example, McDougall maintains there is a parental instinct in man, the corresponding emotion being the tender emotion. But when a child is in danger it is possible, and indeed likely, that the parent will also experience fear; when the child is successful in some enterprise the parent may experience elation and so on.

Thus the child arouses in the parent not only the parental instinct but also other instincts, or at least the affective parts of other instincts.

(6) An instinctive reaction may be detached from the type of object which naturally arouses it, and attached to some other type of object. This type of modification has been much used and discussed by psychiatrists, to whom it is known as sublimation. A typical example is where the instinct of pugnacity is detached from the situation where it is 'naturally' aroused and attached to some social evil, one of the clearest cases being the Salvation Army. But it is also important to educationists, for, by this method, ideas, unconnected with instincts, may provide strong incentives toward action. Thus it is well known that the most powerful incentive among research workers is simply the instinct of curiosity, and it is therefore one of the duties of a teacher to modify that instinct in such a way that the instinctive reaction may be obtained not only when the pupil is confronted by ideas of objects which naturally arouse it, as in (1), but by ideas of a completely different sort such as mathematical ones.

We now come to two types of action which can be modified to a very great extent by the educationist. The first of these is the type of action which is commonly said to be under the control of the individual's intelligence. Such behaviour is not completely modifiable by the educationist, for it is common knowledge that some individuals can never be made to behave as intelligently as others. On the other hand, it is certainly modifiable to a very much greater extent than instinctive behaviour.

Whatever difficulties may be bound up in the conception of instinct, they are certainly trifling when compared with those involved in the conception of intelligence. Broadly speaking, we may say that there are two uses of the word in ordinary life. In the first, intelligence denotes a characteristic by which the individual reacts successfully to his environment; and in the second, intelligence denotes some characteristic of the individual's mental processes. Psychological definitions have ranged roughly from one extreme to the other. Behaviourists tend to use the word in the first sense and other psychologists in the second. This is hardly the place to embark on a discussion of various psychological theories, and I fear the behaviourists will read no further, for I do not propose to say anything about the first use of the word. I agree that intelligence is often used in this sense of successful reaction to environment, but I think that 'successful' must be explained either in terms of reflexes, instincts and habits,[1] or in terms of thought processes; and if it is explained in the former terms I see no reason for the introduction of a new word such as 'intelligence'. Those psychologists who have argued in favour of a behaviourist definition have generally ruled out the kind of phenomenon in which we are really interested. They have spent most of their time watching rats running in mazes, and the more quickly a rat learned to get the bait at

[1] For a discussion of habits, see below, pp. 96–104.

the end of the maze the more intelligent it was considered. If a rat suddenly decided to stop its hectic rush, to sit down in the middle of the maze and to contemplate life, the experiment was discarded as irrelevant. But there is no need of any conception such as intelligence to explain the fact that some rats get the bait more quickly than others, while there is need of such a conception in the analysis of certain mental processes. Thus I shall make no apology for using the word with reference only to mental processes.

Intelligence in this sense is generally defined with reference to mental abilities—an ability being something which the individual can do. But as it is possible to tell what an individual can do only by observation of what he actually does, intelligence becomes more or less a list of tasks which the individual has performed at various times. It is clearly impossible for the list to include everything which the individual has done, and the main problem is to decide what tasks should be included. It would be possible to give a description of the kind of task to be included that would imply that I was more intelligent than Professor Einstein. If such a *reductio ad absurdum* is to be avoided, we must attempt to analyse those abilities which we consider are involved in the mental processes of the individuals whom everyone admits to be the most intelligent. Unfortunately, psychologists are not agreed what these abilities are, but it seems to me that until some agreement is obtained on this question, much of the work done by experimental educationists on intelligence and intelligence testing, however valuable, will remain unappreciated by the average man and by specialists in other subjects.

It must not be thought, however, that agreement is entirely lacking among psychologists. For example, Thorndike introduced what he called 'intellect $CAVD$', where C stood for tasks requiring completion, A stood for arithmetical tasks, V stood for tasks requiring knowledge of vocabulary, and D for tasks requiring the understanding of directions, and it was found that intelligence in this sense had a high correlation with intelligence as ordinarily understood. Moreover, there is no doubt that most psychologists have agreed to a very great extent with Thorndike in this respect, as can be seen from an examination of any current 'intelligence test'. But it seems to me there are two weaknesses in this line of approach. The first is that I do not think it avoids the *reductio ad absurdum* mentioned above. It seems to me to be quite possible that I could obtain as high a score as Professor Einstein could in $CAVD$. Psychologists, when confronted with an objection such as this, generally say that Einstein's outstanding achievements are not perhaps due to an intelligence in excess of mine but to the possession of other mental characteristics. This seems to me to be just absurd. If intelligence means anything at all in ordinary life, it certainly means what Einstein has to a greater degree than I, and if psychologists do not agree, then they are using the word in a way different from its ordinary use. The second weakness in this line of approach is that the selection of tasks in $CAVD$ appears to be arbitrary. There is no attempt to consider what abilities are involved in, for example, an arithmetical task, and to consider whether such abilities are part of what we mean by intelligence.

When we reflect on our own mental processes I think we can see that we possess certain very general intellectual abilities or powers and certain very much more specialized abilities. The general abilities are the abilities to abstract, to retain, to contrast, to compare, etc. For example, if an individual judges 'this pillarbox is red', 'this pack of cards is red', 'this rose is red', and so on, it is clearly unnecessary to endow him with a special ability which enables him to make each judgement. All that is necessary is to endow him with the general powers of retentiveness and abstraction. These general intellectual powers are certainly part of what we ordinarily mean by intelligence, and they are certainly part of what psychologists mean when they test intelligence. For example, many questions in the Stanford revision of the Binet tests are designed to test solely such abilities. Indeed, the general powers appear to me to form what might be called a definition of mind. If we consider, by way of comparison, a piece of matter, such as an iron bar, in the physical world we can distinguish two sorts of properties. The first sort consists of those very general properties which follow from the definition of 'matter', such as weight, volume, etc. The second sort consists of those much more specialized properties such as hardness, magnetization, elasticity, and so on, which it possesses in virtue of the fact that it is a bar of iron and not a pint of beer or some other constituent of the physical world. Similarly, I think such general powers as retentiveness, abstraction, etc., belong to anything that may reasonably be said to possess a mind and may thus form at least part of any definition of mind. Also I think it is true that the more developed such powers or abilities are, the more intelligent the individual is said to be. If that is so, there ought to be universal agreement about part of the nature of intelligence, and every attempt to test intelligence ought to test in part such general abilities.

There are also, however, some much more specialized abilities, and in the following account of these, which is extremely tentative, I wish to acknowledge the help I have received from Mr W. E. Johnson's *Logic*. The first of these specialized abilities is the ability to conduct the ordinary deductive reasoning processes. By 'the ordinary deductive reasoning processes' I mean such a process as is involved in passing to the conclusion of a syllogism from the premises, or, on a higher level, the processes involved in *Principia Mathematica*. Most psychologists have agreed that the ability to reason deductively is a necessary part of intelligence, but I do not think that intelligence tests have tested this ability properly. For the nature of the tests generally excludes an opportunity for the subject justifying his answer. The subject has to find the answer that is as a matter of fact correct, but has not to give any reason. Yet it is the type of reasoning involved in solving a problem that is traditionally thought to be most important. Mathematicians and logicians have always stressed the value of an 'elegant proof', and in ordinary life we should certainly judge a person unintelligent if he had to perform amazing feats of mental acrobatics to deduce the simplest conclusions.

The second of these specialized abilities is the ability to conduct reasoning processes involving problematic induction. This type of reasoning is called induction because in it a universal conclusion is drawn from particular premises, and it is called problematic because the conclusion is not asserted to be certainly true, but is asserted to have such and such a probability. Thus if an event a has been found to occur on every occasion on which conditions A were present, the conclusion that a always occurs under conditions A may be asserted to be probably true, the probability depending on the number of occasions observed, and on the prior probability of a's occurrence. This type of inference is dealt with at length in text-books on probability and inductive inference. Now it seems to me a serious weakness of most discussions of intelligence and intelligence testing that they make no mention of this ability to carry out problematic induction. For there is no doubt that we all use such inferences in ordinary life much oftener than completely certain deductive inferences—for example, we assess the chance of there being rain when we go for a walk. Indeed, we use problematic induction whenever we assess the chance of the future resembling the past. Moreover, in ordinary life if a person does balance chances against each other in a ridiculous manner he is considered unintelligent, even if all his deductive inferences should be scrupulously correct.

The third ability which I think must be included in intelligence is the ability to use what Johnson calls 'intuitive induction'. Propositions established by intuitive induction are universal generalizations from particular premises, but are nevertheless certain. For example, if I am presented with a single instance of red, orange, and yellow, I may make the universal judgement that the qualitative difference between red and yellow is greater than that between red and orange. This judgement has been made on the strength of a single instance, but is nevertheless certainly true. Similarly, from the instance that 3 times 2 feet + 3 times 5 feet = 3 times (2 feet + 5 feet), we may arrive by intuitive induction at the algebraic distributive law

$$ab + ac = a\,(b + c).$$

This ability does not appear at a low level of intelligence, but I think it is always present in individuals who are ordinarily called intelligent, and it ought certainly to be taken account of in any analysis of intellectual ability.

The fourth of these specialized abilities is the ability to symbolize or to form concepts of what has not been presented in sense experience. This is sometimes called by philosophers the ability to form a priori concepts. The development of science especially has shown what tremendous advances have taken place when an adequate symbol or concept has been introduced. But in a smaller way we all, in so far as we are intelligent, use this ability. For example, the conception of cause must be formed by every individual of reasonable intelligence, yet this conception is not presented in sense experience, as all we directly experience is regularity of sequence. Hence it is not a conception which can be formed by any of the general intellectual abilities, such as abstraction, operating on our sense experience, but must be formed by some much more specialized ability. Also I think it is clear that if an individual were quite unable to form such a concept he would be called unintelligent.

These four abilities—the abilities to use deduction, problematic induction, intuitive induction, and the ability to form a priori concepts—seem to me to be an essential part of what is ordinarily meant by intelligence, and I think it is in these four abilities that individuals who differ considerably in intelligence differ most. No doubt there are considerable differences between individuals in the general abilities of abstraction, retentiveness, etc., but I think there is little doubt that the greatest difference between, for example, Professor Einstein and me lies in the fact that Einstein has much greater abilities of what I have called the specialized kind. It is probable that these specialized abilities do not develop for some time in the child, and before they appear it will be necessary to test intelligence by testing the general abilities of the child. But that is no reason for ignoring them in the analysis of intelligence after they have appeared, and I think it probable that if tests could be devised which did test these four more specialized abilities the general public and specialists in other subjects would be more sympathetic to the findings of experimental educationists. The old-fashioned school and university examinations did this to some extent.

This analysis of the nature of intelligence also throws light, I think, on the problem of transfer of training. It has generally been found that when careful experiments have been made, very little transfer takes place. Yet the vast majority of teachers do believe that in some sense or other subjects such as Latin and mathematics have high 'disciplinary value', and that something is transferred from them to other situations. Is it possible to reconcile these two positions? I think to a certain extent it is. If the above account of the nature of intelligence is reasonably accurate, it follows that if an individual's general power of abstraction, for example, is improved, he will appear to be more intelligent. It is natural to suppose that such a power will be improved by some subjects of study more than by others, and in particular will probably be improved by the study of mathematics, if mathematics is taught in such a way that the power will be consciously exercised. This seems to be borne out by recent investigations. 'The conclusion seems to be that transfer of training depends on the conscious acceptance by the learner of "methods", "procedures", "principles", "sentiments", "ideals" and schemata or patterns of thought.'[1] I think this can be put into our language as follows. If the pupil is taught consciously to develop the abilities into which we have analysed intelligence, then these abilities will be improved and consequently transfer will take place. But everything depends on the way in which each subject is taught. It is clearly possible that geography may be taught in such a way that these abilities are developed more than they are by some methods of teaching Latin and mathematics. But I think the opinion of most teachers is probably correct, that if Latin and mathematics are properly taught, then they are the ideal subjects for improving the intelligence.

The intelligence of any individual can therefore be developed to a considerable extent by the educationist, and those actions which are under the control of the intelligence correspondingly modified. But intelligence, as we all know from experience, is not completely under the control of the educationist. No matter what education I had received I could never have done the work of Einstein. It remains for us to consider one further type of action which is completely modifiable by training. This type may conveniently be called habitual, and such actions learned responses or habits, in contrast to physiological actions or reflexes which are perfect at birth and are thus called unlearned responses.

The laws, often called the laws of learning, which govern our learned responses are not always the same, and it is

1 H. R. Hamley, Appendix v, *Spens Report on Secondary Education*.

convenient to start with the famous 'conditioned response'. Pavlov found that if a dog is given something to eat (in the experiments it was usually a piece of meat), one of the unlearned responses, in fact an ordinary reflex action, was an increased flow of saliva from the salivary glands. Each time the meat was presented to the dog a bell was rung, and the whole procedure was repeated on very many occasions. It was eventually found that when the bell was rung in the absence of any food, a salivary response was, nevertheless, obtained from the dog. This response to the bell is what is called a conditioned response; that is, the salivary response is the unconditioned (or unlearned) response to the stimulus of the meat, but the conditioned response to the stimulus of the bell. Pavlov made many experiments of this kind and was able to establish the existence of many conditioned responses. His experiments have been repeated by other psychologists, and the results may now be considered completely established both for animals and human beings.

The laws which govern the conditioning of responses are as follows:

(1) A conditioned response cannot be formed if the stimulus to which the response is the natural response takes place in time before the stimulus to which the response is the conditioned response. For example, if the meat were given to the dog before the bell was rung, no conditioning would take place.

(2) A conditioned response can often be extinguished

in two ways: (*a*) It obeys what is sometimes called the law of forgetting, that is, its strength decreases if it is not periodically exercised. It is generally found, however, that even when forgetting has occurred the response can be re-established much more easily than if it had never been established. (*b*) If the stimulus to which the conditioned response is the natural response does not follow the conditioning stimulus on a number of successive occasions, then the response will eventually not be obtained. That is, if the bell is rung on a number of successive occasions but no meat is presented to the dog, then eventually a time will come such that when the bell is rung no salivary response is obtained. It seems, however, that there are some conditioned responses which cannot be extinguished in either of these ways.

(3) A conditioned response cannot be obtained by any stimulus other than the one to which it has been conditioned. For example, if the response is conditioned to the ringing of the bell, then it will not be obtained by any stimulus other than that.

(4) In general a conditioned response can be established much more rapidly in young animals than in old, in children than in adults, in normal children than in feeble-minded.

(5) A conditioned response cannot be established without the participation of the brain. Pavlov found that when the cerebral hemispheres of a dog had been removed no conditioned reflexes could be obtained. (It will be remembered that some reflex actions can be obtained without the

participation of the brain.) Lashley[1] has made many experiments in this region, and has shown that if parts of the cerebral matter are removed the rate at which responses can be conditioned depends on the amount of matter left intact.

Many habitual actions in man are due to conditioned responses. They range from the extreme case of Dr Rivers's patient, who would rather dodge shells than take cover, to the simple cases of learning the meanings of words. Rivers's patient, as a child, had been frightened by a dog in a narrow 'close', and the response of fear had been conditioned to the stimulus of any small narrow building. Children in the same way become conditioned to the meanings of words. The sound of its mother saying 'doll' makes the child respond in imitation with the sound 'doll'. If the mother at the same time shows the child a doll, the sound response becomes conditioned, or will after a few trials, to the sight of the doll, and on future occasions the child will name the object correctly. Conditioned responses are often easily established by using a painful stimulus, and this was the basis of the old flogging method in teaching. If such a method is used with skill, it will no doubt produce many excellent habits in children, but it should be remembered that the changes which education has to produce in behaviour are not all habitual, and that we do not expect children to resemble the poorer type of circus animal. If we did then the flogging method would be hard to beat.

[1] K. S. Lashley, *Brain Mechanisms and Intelligence*.

The nervous mechanism by which conditioned responses are established is by no means clear, but from the educationist's point of view it is not important. If the reader is interested, he should consult the works of Pavlov, Lashley, Adrian, etc.

Although the conditioned response is the basis of much habitual behaviour, it is almost certain that it is not the basis of all such behaviour. Other ways in which habits are considered to be acquired are by 'trial and error' and by 'insight'. The method of learning by trial and error has been exhaustively discussed by Thorndike and others, but there still appear to be some difficulties. The method is supposed to explain how we acquire such a habit as being able to swing a golf club. The first law governing this type of learning is the Law of Frequency or 'practice makes perfect'. 'When a modifiable connexion between a situation and a response is made, that connexion's strength is, other things being equal, increased. When a modifiable connexion is not made between a situation and a response over a length of time, that connexion's strength is decreased.' It is probable that this is due to the fact that the repeated passage of an impulse along a path in the nervous system tends to break down or weaken the resistances at the synapses and hence to make it easier for succeeding impulses to pass. This law by itself, however, is clearly unable to explain how we learn to swing a golf club. For when any individual starts to play golf he makes many errors. Therefore by this law it would be easier for him to make them a second time, still easier a third time, and so on. Thus it would be impossible to explain how any individual could ever improve his swing. What seems to be needed is some law which entails that the wrong movements get gradually weeded out and the right movements strengthened. Thorndike's Law of Effect (or, as it is sometimes called, the Law of Satisfaction and Annoyance) is such a law. 'When a modifiable connexion between a situation and a response is made and is accompanied or followed by a satisfying state of affairs, that connexion's strength is increased; when made and accompanied or followed by an annoying state of affairs, its strength is decreased.' For example, if an individual makes an unsuccessful swing, his annoyance tends to prevent the movements he made being repeated; if he makes a successful swing, his satisfaction tends to strengthen the movements he made. Such a law is consistent with our ordinary experience, for it is a commonplace that if a person plays badly at golf but is quite content, then he is unlikely to improve. The first essential for improvement is dissatisfaction. But there is still a difficulty in explaining this type of learning by these two laws. The satisfaction which attends a successful drive occurs after the swing has taken place, and it is difficult to see how it could then strengthen connexions which had preceded it in time. Similarly, the dissatisfaction that attends an unsuccessful drive occurs after the swing has taken place, and it is difficult to see how it could then help to weed out the unsuccessful movements which have preceded. It is possible, of course, that there is a peculiar type of causation associated with satisfaction and dissatisfaction which makes it all quite reasonable, but I think it must be admitted that such a possibility runs counter to all our other experience. But Thorndike has a third law, called the Law of Readiness, governing this type of learning. 'When any conduction unit is in readiness to conduct, for it to do so is satisfying. When any conduction unit is not in readiness to conduct, for it to conduct is annoying. When any conduction unit is in readiness to conduct, for it not to do so is annoying.'

If this third law is taken in conjunction with the Law of Effect, it seems possible to eliminate the difficulty about satisfaction. The two laws together assert that if a system of neurones is ready to act and if it does act then the strength of that connexion is increased; on the other hand, if a system of neurones is not ready to act and if it does act, or if it is ready to act and if it does not act, then the strength of that connexion is decreased. This brings in the rather vague conception of the neurones 'being ready to act', but it seems that something of the sort certainly occurs. Moreover, if it is remembered that a nervous impulse is possibly a chemical change which travels along the nerve, it is natural to suppose that when the neurones are 'ready to act' there may be some peculiar chemical change at the synapses. The possibility of this being brought about by means of hormonic action has been suggested by Professor G. H. Thomson.[1] If that is so, it is not unreasonable to

1 G. H. Thomson, *Instinct, Intelligence and Character*, pp. 71–2.

suppose that when the first chemical change is followed by the second (the nervous impulse), the probability that the second chemical change will occur again is increased. It will probably not be long before such problems are finally solved, but whatever their solution may be, it is unlikely that any serious modification will be found necessary in Thorndike's three laws. These laws can be substantially verified by each individual from observation of his own and other people's behaviour.

There is one other method by which learned responses are alleged to be obtained. This is by 'insight'. In experiments on apes Yerkes[1] found that often the ape made no real progress in solving a simple problem for some time, but that after one right choice the ape appeared to have mastered the problem completely and never made a mistake again. This type of observation has been confirmed by other psychologists, for example, by Köhler,[2] and there are certainly plenty of analogous cases to be seen among children in a classroom. The question is not really whether this so-called learning by insight occurs, but whether it is different from the previous type of learning. May it not just be that the learning has occurred very rapidly? Moreover, it is perhaps unfair to say that the ape made no real progress in solving the problem for some time. If a child is learning to swim, there is a considerable period during which the casual observer might say no real progress was

1 R. M. Yerkes, *The Mental Life of Monkeys and Apes*.
2 W. Köhler, *The Mentality of Apes*.

being made, and after the child had succeeded in doing half a dozen strokes the same observer might say, 'Ah! Now he has seen how to do it.' But clearly the period during which no apparent progress was being made was necessary, and the alleged insight would not have occurred without it. Similarly, it is possible that the apparently random exertions of the ape may have been necessary for the alleged act of insight to occur, and when a child appears to solve a short task quickly by insight, it is possible that the trial and error process has merely been reduced to a minimum. Thus I do not think it has been conclusively established that acts of learning by insight are essentially different from acts of the previous type of learning. If indeed they are, the only consequence for educationists will be that they will have to learn and apply whatever laws are found to hold of this third type of learning.

That concludes all that I have to say about the scale of behaviour from unmodifiable to modifiable. It will be remembered that we started with types of action which were quite unmodifiable and we have ended with habitual behaviour, which is behaviour that has been entirely modified through action by the environment. It is this distinction between modifiable and unmodifiable that seems to me to be important for the educationist, but it is generally a different though very similar distinction that is discussed in text-books on educational theory, namely, the distinction between types of behaviour that are due to heredity and types of behaviour that are not due to heredity.

Theoretically there are four possibilities open for a given type of behaviour: (*a*) that it is unmodifiable by education and that it is due to heredity, (*b*) that it is modifiable by education and that it is due to heredity, (*c*) that it is unmodifiable by education and that it is not due to heredity, and (*d*) that it is modifiable by education and that it is not due to heredity. Physiological and reflex behaviour belong to class (*a*), because we have seen that they cannot be modified to any appreciable extent and everyone agrees that in some sense of 'hereditary' they are hereditary. Instinctive and intelligent behaviour belong to class (*b*), because there is general agreement that they also are hereditary in some sense or other. The only type of behaviour which belongs to class (*c*) is the general class of actions which are imposed by the environment, such as actions imposed by gravity. Habits belong to class (*d*), for it is generally, but not universally, held that they are not hereditary. The existence of these four classes shows that the distinction between modifiable and unmodifiable types of behaviour should not be confused with the distinction between hereditary and non-hereditary behaviour. I have said that it is the former distinction that appears to me to be important for the educationist, but as it is possible that some day the educationist may have more direct control of social life than he has at present, it is perhaps desirable to say something about the latter.

Unfortunately, 'hereditary' appears to be a somewhat ambiguous term. The first clear meaning of it is the sense in which it is applied to characteristics which are transmitted according to Mendel's Laws. Gregor Mendel (1822–84), who was a monk in a monastery at Brünn, experimented with different varieties of the ordinary edible pea. He crossed a pure tall variety with a pure short variety and found that the first generation, which we shall call G_1, was all tall. The first generation was allowed to self-fertilize and the second generation, which we shall call G_2, was found to be composed of both tall and short in the approximate ratio of three talls to one short. Mendel explained these results in the following way. Suppose that in the original tall strain there are two 'elements' which correspond to tallness, and similarly that in the original short strain there are two 'elements' which correspond to shortness. Suppose that in each member of any generation there is one element from each of the parent strains, but suppose that an element for tallness always 'dominates' an element for shortness (or that an element for shortness is 'recessive' to an element for tallness). If t and s stand for the tall and short elements respectively we may denote the original pure strains by (t, t) and (s, s) and the hybrid G_1 by (t, s). If now G_1 is allowed to self-fertilize, there are four equally probable combinations for G_2, namely, (t, t), (t, s), (s, t), (s, s). Because t dominates s, three of these will be tall and one short, which is in fact the observed ratio of talls to shorts in G_2.

Mendel's explanation may be subjected to various further tests. Suppose the hybrid G_1 is crossed with the original short strain. That is, (t, s) is crossed with (s, s). The equally probable combinations are (t, s), (t, s), (s, s), (s, s), which gives an equal ratio of talls and shorts. This has been found to be true. Moreover, the results obtained for the pea apply in general to other organisms, provided that in place of tallness and shortness we take any pair of characters which appear in the organism as alternatives (for example, brown eyes and blue eyes in man).

Mendel's investigations have been rapidly extended by great advances in our knowledge of the physiology of sexual reproduction. It has been found that a large part of the nucleus of the human reproductive cell consists of a substance called chromatin. Just before a fertilized ovum divides into two cells, the chromatin can be observed to consist of microscopic 'rods' which are called chromosomes. In the human female cell there are 48 chromosomes arranged in 24 pairs, in the human male cell there are 47 chromosomes plus what appears to be a portion of one. This portion is generally denoted by Y and is partner to an ordinary sized chromosome generally called X. Hence the human male cell has 23 pairs of chromosomes plus the pair (X, Y), the human female cell has 23 pairs of chromosomes plus the pair (X, X). The chromosomes X and Y are called sex chromosomes, a pair (X, X) giving a female and a pair (X, Y) giving a male. When the life of a new individual begins, each of the reproductive cells discards one of each pair of chromosomes—which one it is appears to be a matter of pure chance. Since each cell had originally

24 paired chromosomes there will be left in each 24 single chromosomes, and during the act of fusion these unite and again form 24 paired chromosomes. The pair (X, X) in the female necessarily contributes an X chromosome to the new individual; the pair (X, Y) in the male may contribute either an X or a Y. Hence in the new individual we obtain either (X, X) a girl, or, with equal chances, (X, Y) a boy.

From this evidence it was a short step to suppose that Mendel's 'elements' were associated with a pair of like chromosomes in the reproductive cells, and this has been conclusively demonstrated to be true by subsequent research. In fact, we can now say that the elements are associated with certain parts of the chromosomes called 'genes',[1] so that genes may be regarded as the units of heredity.

We can therefore say that a type of behaviour is hereditary in the first sense if it is due to some characteristic of the individual which is transmitted in accordance with Mendel's Laws. Unfortunately, the list of human characteristics which are known to be transmitted in this way is not very long. It includes, among others, eye colour, haemophilia, a type of insanity known as Huntington's chorea, and at least one form of colour blindness. There is also some evidence that feeble-mindedness behaves as a Mendelian recessive character, but considerably more investigation is required. It is possible, and indeed likely, that many more human characteristics will eventually be found

[1] T. H. Morgan, *The Theory of the Gene*.

to obey Mendel's Laws, but at present we are not entitled to say that most human characteristics are transmitted in this way.

A second meaning of heredity that educationists use when they talk about hereditary types of behaviour is as follows. It is found that there are certain structures of the human body which are essential causal factors in the production of some types of behaviour. For example, the glands are such factors with respect to temperamental behaviour, and the nervous system is such a factor with respect to reflex behaviour. Now these structures are present in all normal human bodies, and the types of behaviour are consequently called 'innate' or 'hereditary'. That is, a type of behaviour is hereditary in this second sense if there exists some structure found in all human bodies which is an essential causal factor in its production. In this sense it is clear that physiological, temperamental and reflex behaviour are hereditary. Can we say that instinctive and intelligent behaviour are hereditary in this sense, for they are generally claimed to be hereditary in some sense? It seems to me that instinctive behaviour (in the sense in which we have used it) is certainly not hereditary in this sense. McDougall, as far as I know, never made any attempt to correlate any anatomical structures with his various instincts. There is, however, much more plausibility in supposing that intelligent behaviour is hereditary in this sense, and Thorndike's Quantity Hypothesis[1] immediately sug-

1 E. L. Thorndike, *The Measurement of Intelligence*, chap. xv.

gests itself. According to this 'the higher forms of intellectual operation are identical with mere association or connexion forming, depending upon the same sort of physiological connexions but requiring many more of them'.[1] 'Any person familiar with the finer anatomy of the brain will at once think of the number of possible contacts (or possibly coalescences) of the fibrils of axones with dendritic processes in the associative neurones.'[2] I do not think it can be yet claimed that Thorndike's view must be accepted, but if it is then intelligence is hereditary in this second sense.

There is still, however, a third sense in which a type of behaviour is sometimes said to be hereditary. It is found that members of the same species often exhibit uniformities of behaviour even when all opportunities of learning have been carefully excluded. Such uniformities are then said to be hereditary types of behaviour. For example, the young of certain species perform some types of behaviour which their parents performed even although the latter die before the young are able to learn. In the human species, instincts (in McDougall's and our use of the word) are hereditary in this third sense; for clearly individuals do exhibit uniformities in what we called their instinctive reactions, and in a large number of cases no opportunity of learning such reactions has been afforded.

The question as to whether learned responses or habits are hereditary has caused a good deal of discussion. The

1 Thorndike, op. cit. p. 415.   2 Op. cit. p. 422.

early biologists, and common sense as well, held that they were. But Weismann, who lived shortly after Charles Darwin, produced a great deal of evidence to show that they were not, and until recently his view was generally accepted. If it is true it follows that the benefits and misfortunes conferred on individuals by education are not transmitted biologically but must be conferred anew on each generation. Recently, however, a few investigators have claimed to have found evidence that contradicts Weismann's view. It cannot be said that the question is finally settled, but it seems to me that the distinctions we have drawn between the different meanings of 'hereditary' may clarify the issue a little.

Evidence has been obtained that the environment is sometimes able to cause changes in the chemical or structural constitution of the genes in the germ cells. If a new individual is formed from such cells, these changes will cause a new character to appear, and such a character (and the behaviour due to it) will be hereditary. Unfortunately, it is not at all clear what causes these changes or mutations, as they are technically called. Short-wave radiation may be one of the causes, but that hardly exists in sufficient intensity to explain even those mutations which are known to have occurred. Whatever may be the cause, however, it is logically possible that the acquisition of certain habits *might* cause changes in the germ cells which *might* produce a new character in the offspring, and that such a character *might* cause in the offspring the same habitual behaviour as in the parent. As far as I know there is no evidence that the acquisition of any habit does produce mutations, but it is possible that some such cases may be discovered, and if they were then it would be true to say that such learned responses were hereditary.

When most biologists assert conclusively that acquired responses are not transmitted by heredity I think what they mean is something different. The sense of heredity they are using is either the second or the third. For example, if an individual acquires a new type of behaviour because of the amputation of a leg, such behaviour is not transmitted—even if many generations have a leg amputated and even if each of these generations acquires the same type of be- haviour. Thus habits are not hereditary in the second sense. Similarly, if one generation of a species learns a certain type of behaviour it is always found that the next generation has also to learn it, that is, there is no evidence that habits are hereditary in the third sense. (McDougall at one time claimed to have evidence that some habits of rats were hereditary in this third sense, but it was not regarded as satisfactory.)

In brief, then, I think we can say the position is as follows. There are three senses in which a type of human behaviour may be hereditary. The only types that can be said definitely to be hereditary in the first sense are certain abnormalities, although it is possible that more research will prove other types to be hereditary also in this sense. Physiological, temperamental, and reflex behaviour are hereditary in the second sense, and intelligent behaviour is also probably hereditary in this sense. Instinctive behaviour is hereditary in the third sense. Habitual behaviour is not hereditary in either the second or the third sense, but it is possible that, under certain conditions, it may be so in the first sense. If it is, these conditions have not yet been found. The improvement of the human race, through suitable selection, in the types of behaviour that are hereditary, and the improvement, through education, in the types of behaviour that are not hereditary, and in the types which, though hereditary, are nevertheless modifiable, are the two greatest needs not only of the present but of all time.

This leads us to the consideration of what is perhaps the most important of the conceptions in the definition of education—the idea of value, because on that depends what changes we decide should be produced in the child. It is true, I think, that most of the disagreement between education theorists arises over this conception. The only types of theory in which this is not so have already been dealt with, namely, nature theories which hold a peculiar and, as I think, wrong conception of the original nature of man and of the way in which changes of behaviour may be produced, and Dewey's theory which attempts to exclude (but does not succeed in doing so) the conception of value. Of the theories which disagree about this last conception some hold that the changes in behaviour should be directed towards an end such as 'citizenship', others towards an end such as 'happiness', and so on. Of such theories there is one that must be considered at once, for if it is right all the others are certainly wrong, and I do not think that some educationists have quite realized the strength of its case. The theory in question may conveniently be called a religious theory of education. It holds that the nature of the environment in the most general sense, that is, the nature of the universe, implies that there exists a Being who created life for some definite purpose. If so, then the value of the changes which education has to produce in each individual must be judged by the extent to which they enable each individual to fulfil that purpose. The main problem, if such a view of education is correct, is to find out what that purpose is, and the supporters of the different religious faiths all attempt to give an answer to this problem. What we must briefly consider here, however, is how far the general nature of the environment does justify the conclusion that life was created for some definite purpose. For I think it is true that if the conclusion is justified then our idea of value and hence our whole conception of education must conform to that conclusion.[1]

The argument in favour of a religious theory of education is roughly as follows. It is now known that the solar system is the result of an accident. Some thousand million years ago a star happened to approach close to the sun. This star, as it approached, raised enormous tides on the sun and,

---

[1] For example, I think some, or perhaps all, Christians would hold that the habits formed by education must be such as will help to prepare the individual for eternal life. Plato held a similar view.

as it passed, a portion, in the form of a sausage, was torn out of the sun. This portion soon broke up into separate bits, and as they solidified these different bits became the planets. This implies that life must have come to the earth. For water is a necessary constituent of all organisms known to us, and if the earth was originally at the same temperature as the sun, then the existence of organisms on it was originally impossible. For organisms to exist there must be a permanent temperature lower than the boiling-point of water. Thus we can say quite definitely that the earth was once lifeless. How then did life appear? There are three logical possibilities. (1) Life may have come from some region outside the earth. (2) There may have been a specific creative act. (3) Life may have made its appearance from non-living material.

The first possibility can, I think, be rejected. If it were true, it would follow that small primitive organisms must have been transmitted through space from some body on which life was already present, but it seems practically certain that conditions existing in intrastellar space are such as to make the existence of life quite impossible. Thus there must either have been a specific creative act or life must have developed from the non-living. The latter view implies that if we could reproduce in a laboratory the conditions under which life first developed from the non-living, then we could again cause it to appear. So far all such attempts have failed. Also the argument that some specific creative act was necessary is strengthened by the fact that the conditions necessary for life had rather remarkably been brought about. The three fundamental elements of organic chemistry are hydrogen, oxygen and carbon, and from these elements are built up the molecules which are the chemical basis of organisms. Because of the remarkable supply of hydrogen, oxygen and carbon with which the first organism would find itself surrounded, it would have plenty of food and more complex organisms could then be developed. Thus there is no doubt that 'carbon, hydrogen, and oxygen, each by itself, and all taken together, possess unique and pre-eminent chemical fitness for the organic mechanism. They alone are best fitted to form it and to set it in motion; and their stable compounds water and carbonic acid, which make up the changeless environment, protect and renew it, forever drawing fresh energy from the sunshine.'[1]

On the other hand, it is certainly false to state that a specific creative act must have occurred. Living things have great adaptability, and if the environment had not abounded with carbon, hydrogen and oxygen it is possible that some other elements might have been used instead. Moreover, the original development of an organism from some extremely complex molecule could clearly have been a matter of chance. It is true that we do not seem to find such events occurring now, that is, we do not find life appearing of itself from non-living matter. But it must be remembered that the chance of it appearing even once may

1 L. J. Henderson, *The Fitness of the Environment*, p. 248.

be so small that it would be surprising if it did appear a second time. For example, it is physically possible that molecules of matter might by chance take up the position which they have in a Ford motor car, even to the extent of having petrol in the tank and an ignition key on the switchboard. Everyone would agree, however, that the chance of such an event is extraordinarily small. Now if the chance of atoms arranging themselves in such a way as to produce a molecule capable of developing into an organism was about the same as the chance of molecules arranging themselves in such a way as to produce a Ford car suitably equipped, then we should not be surprised that life has not arisen again. For we certainly have no experience of motor cars being produced by chance. On the other hand, since we can arrange molecules in the way necessary to produce a Ford car, it may yet be possible to arrange atoms in such a way as to produce life.

Hence the conclusion I would suggest is that although the physical environment seems extremely well suited to the production and continuation of life, yet there is no doubt that such production may have been a matter of chance; and the reason that we have no experience of such production now is that the chance is so extraordinarily small. In what follows then I shall assume that the general nature of the environment does not imply that life has been created for some external purpose, and that education must produce those changes which will be useful for that purpose. That is, when educationists hold, for example, that certain habits which it is their business to form in the child are valuable habits, I am going to assume that they do not mean that these habits will enable the child to fulfil the purpose for which life was created.

The problem is what do they mean? It is hardly likely that I shall be able to solve a problem about whose solution educationists, from Plato onwards, have perpetually disagreed. But I think it is important that we should be clear as to what exactly the problem is, and as to what solutions are definitely possible. The educationist has, I think, two problems in this region to solve. The first is, what is meant by such a term as 'good' or 'valuable'? The second is, how do we come to know, and hence how can we teach the meaning of such a term? For the valuable changes in behaviour which education has to secure must include the description of it as such. Education would clearly have partly failed if individuals behaved perfectly but did not know it. The solution of the second problem will, however, probably depend on the solution of the first.

It is important to realize at the outset that 'good' is used in a great many different ways, for example, in the phrases 'a good plumber', 'a good hand at bridge', 'a good garden'. But when people have disputed about the meaning of 'good', the disputes have not always been caused simply by the fact that the parties to the dispute were talking about different things. In such examples as 'a good plumber', etc., it is easy to define 'good' in such a way as to cause no disagreement. For example, 'a good hand at bridge' may be defined as 'a hand that will take many tricks'. Similarly, when educationists have talked about good habits being formed in the child there is no doubt that sometimes they have meant habits useful for this, that, or the next thing. But it is clear that there are some uses of 'good' which cannot be translated so simply. For example, most educationists a century ago would have said that knowledge of Greek literature was good, and would have urged that the behaviour of children be directed accordingly. By this they meant partly that it was useful for various purposes, such as producing an agreeable citizen, but they also meant more than this. They meant that knowledge of Greek literature was good in itself, that is, even if everything else were different, the value of Greek literature would remain unchanged. It is this sense of good-in-itself, or what is sometimes called intrinsically good, that has caused the disagreement among educationists, and it is about this sense that we must attempt to get clear.

Let us then consider briefly the meaning of good in this sense of intrinsically good. Either (a) it is possible that 'good' can be defined in terms of ordinary characteristics by a biverbal definition of the first kind (it could always be defined by a biverbal definition of the second kind, for example, good = valuable); or (b) it is not possible so to define 'good'. Those theories which maintain (a) are generally called naturalistic theories, and those theories which maintain (b) are generally called non-naturalistic theories.

Naturalistic theories, or theories which maintain (*a*), may be of various kinds. Typical examples are the following:

X is good = I desire X (Hobbes).

X is good = X is approved by most people (Hume).

X is good = X tends to promote the stability (or instability) of society (a sociological theory).

X is good = X is approved by God (a theological theory).

X is good = X tends to promote the total pleasure (or happiness) of mankind (a psychological theory).

All such theories can be refuted by the argument due to Moore which was used in Chapter I.[1]

It follows that good in this sense of intrinsically good is indefinable by a biverbal definition of the first kind. If that is so it also follows that we must learn and teach its meaning by means of ostensive definitions. This brings us to the second problem which we have to consider, namely, how do we come to know the meaning of good?

I think we can see what solutions are possible here if we consider what intellectual abilities are involved. It will be remembered that the conception of intelligence was analysed into certain general abilities and four much more specialized abilities: (1) the ability to reason deductively, (2) the ability to use problematic induction, (3) the ability

[1] See p. 17. Moore's argument has often been criticized, but the spirit of it is still sound. It is always an open question whether a thing possessing any of the characteristics suggested is good, and the openness is not due solely to the ambiguity of 'good'. The question is never equivalent to 'is good itself good?'

to form a priori concepts, (4) the ability to use what Johnson calls intuitive induction. Now it is certain that abilities (1) and (2) are employed in learning the meaning of value judgements. For example, ability (1) might be used in deducing possible consequences from a proposed course of behaviour, and ability (2) might be used in arguing that because such and such a habit was good in one situation it would be good in a similar situation. How far is ability (3), that is, the ability to form a priori concepts, used? From Moore's argument it follows that 'good' cannot be defined, but it does not necessarily follow that 'good' is an a priori concept. There are three possibilities: (a) that good is an a priori concept, (b) that it is an empirical concept, (c) a third alternative to be discussed below.

It might be thought that alternative (b) was impossible since 'good' is indefinable, but that is not so. The concept of red, for example, is indefinable by a biverbal definition of the first kind. Its meaning is learned by means of ostensive definitions, that is, by having examples of red things pointed out, and by using the general intellectual powers of comparison, abstraction, etc. Similarly, those moralists who hold that human beings possess 'a moral sense' doubtless hold that we learn the meaning of good in much the same way. Thus alternative (b) is certainly logically possible, and is in fact held by a number of people. If it is accepted it does follow that intelligence in the sense of ability (3) is not used in learning the meaning of value judgements. On the other hand, if alternative (a) is accepted, that good is an a priori concept, then ability (3) is used.

How far is ability (4) involved, that is, how far do we use intuitive induction? Suppose I make the judgement 'all knowledge is good'. There are two possibilities this time. (*a*) It is possible that this is an empirical generalization similar to the generalization 'all water boils at 100° C.' after the observation 'this sample of water boils at 100° C.' (*b*) It is possible that it is a generalization arrived at by intuitive induction, that is, by reflexion on some piece of knowledge I may see a necessary connexion between knowledge and goodness which enables me to judge that all knowledge is good. Both these possibilities are open whether good is an a priori concept or an empirical one. For it is possible to make empirical generalizations involving a priori concepts, for example, germs *cause* disease. If (*a*) is correct then intelligence in the sense of ability (4) is not involved, but if (*b*) is correct then it is involved in learning the meaning of 'good'.

These seem to me to be the various alternatives which are open, and the educationist should adjust the ostensive definitions which he gives according to the alternatives which he accepts. It remains, however, for us to discuss alternative (*c*) mentioned above, as it appears to me to be the one which should be accepted.

When we considered the educational theory of John Dewey, we noted that language was used for a number of purposes of which one was to communicate information.

We have assumed so far that in such a proposition as 'knowledge of Greek literature is good' the intention is to convey information; that is, we have assumed that 'good' is the name of a certain characteristic which we predicate of a number of things or mental states or what not, and we have been attempting to get clearer about the nature of this characteristic. Now I propose to deny this assumption. In other words I do not believe that when we make a proposition such as 'knowledge of Greek literature is good', or any other proposition involving the word 'good' or 'valuable' in this sense of intrinsically good, our intention is to convey information about what it is like to know Greek literature. Our intention is rather to arouse a certain attitude in our audience. The use of language in the way we use it when we convey information is now generally called the *scientific use* of language; and the use of language in the way we use it when we try to arouse an emotional attitude in the hearer, or to influence him in some other way than by giving him information, is generally called the *emotive use* of language. Hence this third alternative about the nature of 'good' is that when we make value judgements we are using language emotively rather than scientifically.

The emotive use of language is seen most clearly in poetry. 'A lyrical poem has no assertational sense, no theoretical sense, it does not contain knowledge.... The aim of a lyrical poem in which occur the words "sunshine" and "clouds" is not to inform us of certain meteorological facts but to express certain feelings of the poet and to excite similar feelings in us.'[1] Similarly, when I make a value judgement I believe that I am expressing certain feelings of my own and am attempting to excite similar feelings in others; that is, a value judgement is both expressive and persuasive. It should be clearly understood that the judgement *expresses* certain feelings and does not *describe* them. Let us consider a parallel case. If I am annoyed, I may describe my feelings by saying 'I am annoyed', or I may express them by saying 'Damn'. Now the sentence 'I am annoyed' is an example of the scientific use of language and can be significantly contradicted, in other words, it is possible that I am lying when I say 'I am annoyed'. But 'Damn' is an example of the emotive use of language and cannot be significantly contradicted, because it does not *state* anything, although it may express a great deal. Similarly, I believe that when I say 'knowledge of Greek literature is valuable' I am expressing my feelings about Greek literature—indeed, I am expressing what is stated by the sentence 'I like Greek literature'.

But it is clear that value judgements must do more than merely express feelings. For we have seen that it is impossible to contradict a purely expressive utterance such as 'Damn', but there is no doubt that people do disagree violently about value judgements, and if each person was merely expressing his own feelings such disagreement would be quite unjustified. This brings us to the second function of value judgements—namely, that they are per-

1 R. Carnap, *Philosophy and Logical Syntax*, pp. 28–9.

suasive. They are an attempt to arouse the same sort of feelings in the audience. Hence the judgement 'knowledge of Greek literature is good' expresses roughly what is stated by 'I like Greek literature and I want you to do so as well'. When two people therefore disagree about the truth of a value judgement, each is attempting to arouse in the other the same sort of feeling which he himself experiences. This seems to me to explain the peculiar nature of controversy about value judgements and the difficulty (sometimes the impossibility) of securing agreement. Although most educationists have not interpreted value judgements in such a way, many parents in practice do accept the above account. 'Consider the case of a mother who says to her several children, "One thing is certain, we all like to be neat". If she really believed this, she wouldn't bother to say so. But she is not using the words descriptively. She is encouraging the children to like neatness. By telling them they like neatness, she will lead them to *make* her statement true, so to speak. If, instead of saying "We all like to be neat" in this way, she had said "It's a good thing to be neat" the effect would have been approximately the same.'[1] If this account is correct, it follows that neither the ability to form a priori concepts, nor the ability to use intuitive induction is involved in learning the meaning of value judgements. This explains reasonably why it is possible for a particular kind of value judgement—moral judgement—to be made

[1] C. L. Stevenson, 'The Emotive Meaning of Ethical Terms', *Mind*, N.S. vol. XLVI, pp. 24–5.

by quite young children. Mr Bertrand Russell, for example, urges that the moral training of children should be practically finished by the time the child is six years of age.[1] If it were true that 'good' was an a priori concept, it would be virtually certain that Russell's view was absurd, for the average child of six years is not intelligent enough to form a priori concepts. But it is clearly possible that the child of six years should have been trained to have certain feelings about objects and situations, and indeed to have learned the use of 'good' so as to influence other people's feelings.

Again, if this account of the nature of value judgements is correct, it follows that the exercise of intelligence is not the only mental process necessary for their formation, but the ability to experience certain emotions is also necessary. A value judgement on this view does not assert that certain emotions are being experienced by an individual or a group of people, but expresses this fact, and clearly it cannot express the fact unless the fact occurs. This affords an explanation of the well-known fact that it is hopeless to teach a child to make value judgements about actions or objects unless the child is in such a situation that he is likely to experience the required emotion.

This account explains also, I think, why there has been so much disagreement among education theorists about what changes in behaviour are valuable, and why that disagreement has not been removed in the course of time in the way in which scientific disagreement is removed.

1 Bertrand Russell, *On Education*, p. 189.

The disagreement has not been in *what* has been said, but in the feelings which each educationist has had for the different activities of life, and each has attempted to persuade others to feel the same way as he does. If we realize this we can be tolerant to all their theories, for no one is right and no one is wrong. It is true that some may be said to be 'better' than others in the sense in which one poem may be better than another, but when we realize that we realize also that much of the sting has gone out of educational controversy.

CHAPTER V

The Theory of Educational Measurement

There is one important part of the educationist's work that has been entirely ignored in the last chapter, and to it we must now turn. This is the field of educational measurement, a field in which almost all the research that is at present going on in education is taking place. In this chapter I propose to consider what might be called the theory of such measurement, by which I mean the presuppositions and the conditions involved when such measurement takes place. Some such inquiry seems to be desirable, for there is little doubt that scientists working in other fields are distrustful of the possibility of educational measurement. This distrust would probably be removed if the results of educational measurement had great practical success, but it must be confessed that so far the results, although not as meagre as many critics maintain, have been disappointing. It is possible, therefore, that an examination of the conditions under which measurement is possible in education may remove such distrust, and may help to secure wider acceptance of those results which have been shown to have practical value.

The difficulty of such an inquiry is increased by the fact that there is no unanimity concerning the conditions under which measurement is possible even in such a subject as physics. The following are typical accounts that have been given:

'The fundamental rules for measurement must now be shortly stated. They are (1) two bodies matching a third with respect to the given property (length, weight) match each other; (2) the addition of objects having the given property increases that property in accordance with the laws of arithmetic; (3) the addition of equals yields equals.'[1]

Johnson's account may be summarized as follows. It must be possible (1) to find a unit magnitude, (2) to make a direct judgement of comparison, (3) to give a meaning to addition of units.[2]

Brown and Thomson say: 'The preconditions of measurement in any sphere of experience are (1) the *homogeneity* of the phenomena, or any particular aspect of it, to be measured, (2) the possibility of fixing a *unit* in terms of which the measurement may be made, and of which the total magnitude may be regarded as a mere multiple or sub-multiple.'[3]

Guilford writes: 'We shall not attempt to formulate a short and comprehensive definition of measurement here. ...It should be sufficient for the sake of discussion to say that in making a measurement we assign numbers to phenomena and those numbers may be added or sub-tracted.'[4]

1 L. S. Stebbing, *A Modern Introduction to Logic*, p. 373.
2 W. E. Johnson, *Logic*, Part II, chap. VII.
3 W. Brown and G. H. Thomson, *Essentials of Mental Measurement*, p. 1.   4 J. P. Guilford, *Psychometric Methods*, pp. 1–2.

One difficulty in all such accounts is that they do not distinguish between two physical properties, such as density and weight, each of which is considered measurable, but which are not measurable in the same sense. Guilford's account, although I do not suggest that he means this, suffers from the further disadvantage that it would apply to telephone numbers on the same exchange, and no one ordinarily considers that these measure anything.

I think it is important to distinguish at the outset what may be called the objective and subjective conditions of measurement. The subjective conditions are those which must be satisfied by the individual who is measuring, and the objective conditions are those which must be satisfied by the property which is measured. The property is then measurable by a given observer if both the subjective and objective conditions are satisfied. For example, in Johnson's account the second condition is subjective, and the first and third objective, while of the conditions given by Stebbing the first conceals subjective conditions by the use of the word 'match'.

There are, I think, three subjective conditions necessary for any measurement to be possible. An observer must be able (1) to make judgements of 'simultaneity', 'before', and 'after' in time; (2) to make judgements of 'coincidence' and 'consecutiveness' in space; (3) to count the number of a group. I think these conditions are fulfilled when any property is called measurable, and the sense in which it is measurable is determined by the nature of the objective conditions satisfied. There are three classes of such conditions which give rise to the three senses of measurement appropriate to what have been called intensive magnitudes, fundamental magnitudes, and derived magnitudes.[1]

Let us take first intensive magnitudes. The objective condition in this case is that the property generates an order in those bodies that possess the property. Now a set of terms can be ordered if there is a relation connecting them that is transitive, asymmetrical, and connected,[2] so that the condition may be expressed alternatively, a property is measurable if it generates a transitive, asymmetrical and connected relation among bodies that possess the property. A physical example is given by Mohs's scale of hardness. Here the relation is 'scratches', that is, if metal A scratches metal B, A is said to be harder than B. There is one slight difficulty, as the relation 'scratches' is not, strictly speaking, connected; for it is possible to find two metals A and B such that neither A scratches B nor B scratches A. Fortunately, however, it is found that two such metals behave towards

1 This is the terminology used by N. R. Campbell in *Physics, The Elements*. The discussion in the next four paragraphs is due entirely to him.

2 A relation is said to be transitive if, when it holds between A and B, and also between B and C, it holds between A and C. For example, 'north of' is a transitive relation. A relation is said to be asymmetrical if when it holds between A and B it never holds between B and A. For example, 'wife of' is an asymmetrical relation. A relation R is said to be connected with respect to a set of terms if given any two terms A and B of the set, either ARB or BRA holds. For example, the relation 'to the right of' is connected with respect to the set of points on a straight line.

all other metals in the same way as regards scratching, so *A* is said to have the same measure of hardness as *B*. In general, when two bodies are assigned the same measure the generating relation is not connected, but as long as the two bodies react to other bodies in the same way an order can always be maintained if we admit that the two bodies may occupy the same place. When metals have been arranged in this way, we can call the softest (or hardest) 1, the next in the series 2, and so on.

The value of such measurement, however, is clearly limited, for the numerals attached to the different metals are, to a large extent, arbitrary. Thus if *A* is harder than *B*, the numeral assigned to *A* must be greater (or less, if the opposite convention is used) than the numeral assigned to *B*. But that is the only restriction and how much greater (or less) is left completely undetermined.

The objective conditions which a property must satisfy when it can be measured as a fundamental magnitude are more interesting. In addition to the condition that the property must generate an order among those bodies that possess it, the two following conditions are necessary. It must be possible to find some process, which may be called 'addition', such that (1) the system *C* produced by this process from two bodies *A* and *B* both of which possess the property in question must be assigned a rank higher than the rank assigned to either *A* or *B*; and (2) the position of *C* in the series of bodies possessing the property must depend only on the positions of *A* and *B* in the series and not on the order or method of their addition. When these conditions are satisfied it is customary to assign to the system C the sum of the numbers assigned to A and to B. Weight and length are obvious examples of properties which are measurable in this sense.

It is clear, however, that intensive magnitudes and fundamental magnitudes are not the only senses in which properties can be measured. For physicists certainly consider density to be measurable. Now the numbers attached to bodies of different densities are not arbitrary in the sense in which the numbers attached to the different metals in Mohs's scale of hardness are arbitrary; also there is no process by which we can combine two bodies to give a body having a density greater than that of either. Hence density is neither an intensive nor a fundamental magnitude. In what sense then is it measurable?

The objective conditions in this case are that not only must the property generate an order among those objects that possess the property, but that there exists also a numerical law which is true of the objects possessing the property. For example, if A, B, and C are three liquids which do not react chemically with each other, and if A floats on B and B floats on C, then A floats on C. Further, if A floats on B, B does not float on A. Hence the relation 'floats on' generates an order among liquids. Moreover, for each liquid a law of the form mass = $k \times$ volume is found to hold where k is a constant for the liquid. Now if these constants for different liquids are arranged in numerical order, the order is found to be the same as that generated by the relation 'floats on'. Hence k (called the density of the liquid) is said to be a derived magnitude. In general, a derived magnitude is a constant occurring in a numerical law such that the order of objects when arranged with respect to this constant is the same as the order when arranged with respect to some intensive magnitude. Density is thus measurable in this sense of derived magnitude.

We may sum up the discussion so far as follows. There are three senses of measurement which occur in physics, and they are distinguished by the objective conditions which are satisfied in each case. The only condition common to them all is that the property which is being measured must generate an order among the objects that possess it, and this is the only condition necessary if the property is an intensive magnitude. If the property is a fundamental magnitude two further conditions involving some operation on the objects possessing the property must be satisfied, and if the property is a derived magnitude the order generated by the property must be the same as the order generated by a constant (associated with each object possessing the property) occurring in some numerical law.

The important question is, then, are the properties which are measured in educational experiments intensive magnitudes, fundamental magnitudes, or derived magnitudes, or is there still another sense in which such properties are measurable? There does not appear to be general agreement among educationists as to the answer to this question.

As far as I know there has been no attempt to show that such properties are measurable in any sense other than the three already discussed. Moreover, it is true that individuals can be ordered with regard to the properties measured in educational experiments, for example, intelligence, hand-writing, etc. I do not think that anyone has disputed that. The question thus reduces to, are the properties which are measured by educationists merely intensive magnitudes or are they fundamental or derived magnitudes?

This question is of great importance, as the mathematical techniques which are to be employed in dealing with the results of experiments depend upon the answer. If measurement is possible only in the sense of intensive magnitudes then it must be remembered that the numbers attached by tests mean no more than the numbers attached to the houses in a street, that is, they merely rank the subjects of the test. The letters of the alphabet would serve almost as well. This has not always been realized. For example, Guilford writes: 'It is sometimes pointed out that the so-called measurements in psychology rest upon ordinal numbers rather than cardinal numbers.... There is much truth in this.... It can be shown, however, that, when a test contains a very large number of items, the increments of difficulty become very small and approach equality. The resulting series of scores may thus approach a status not unlike that in which cardinal numbers apply and the scores may be treated as if they actually were cardinal numbers. This is what mental testers have done, usually without being at all bothered about the logic of the situation.'[1] But if the practical results of the testing movement are not as encouraging as we all desire, it is perhaps time that we did bother about the logic of the situation. If educational measurements are measurements merely of intensive magnitudes, then it follows that most of the calculations which educationists have done are a waste of time. A few will still be of value. For example, if individuals are arranged in order with respect to two different abilities, then Spearman's formula

$$r = 1 - \frac{6\Sigma d^2}{n\left(n^2 - 1\right)},$$

where d is the difference between the ranks of an individual and n is the number of individuals, may be used to find the relationship between the two abilities. If $r = +1$ one ability is a function of the other in the sense that they increase and decrease together. If $r = -1$ one ability is a function of the other in the sense that an increase in the one is accompanied by a decrease in the other. If $r = 0$ then the two abilities are quite independent. For intermediate values of r it is not very clear what r represents, but it seems reasonable to suppose that some law will be found and that r will in some sense measure the relationship between the two abilities. But all calculations which depend not on the relative rank of the individual but on the number associated with him by means of the test will be valueless. It is therefore of great importance for educationists to show that the

1 J. P. Guilford, *Psychometric Methods*, p. 4.

properties which they measure are measurable in some sense other than that of intensive magnitudes.

The most noteworthy attempts to show this have been made by Thorndike[1] and Thurstone[2] with regard to intelligence. Thomson[3] has recently shown that these attempts are essentially equivalent, so we need consider only Thorndike's work. Thorndike's construction of what is called a scale of intelligence of equal units commencing from an absolute zero depends upon the proposition that intelligence is normally distributed throughout the population in any age group. This proposition is assumed not only as regards intelligence but as regards many abilities by a large number of educationists, and very rarely is any attempt made to show that the normal curve is actually the one which fits the experimental evidence best. Thorndike, however, makes no such assumption. Instead, he proceeded in a manner similar to the following for each grade. He obtained eleven frequency tables of the scores made by sixth-grade pupils in many different cities of the U.S.A. from eleven well-known intelligence tests. These distributions were plotted in units of one-tenth of the standard deviation of each distribution, and the individual curves were found to be somewhat irregular in shape. Thorndike

1 E. L. Thorndike, *The Measurement of Intelligence*.
2 L. L. Thurstone, 'A Method of Scaling Psychological and Educational Tests', *Journal of Educational Psychology*, vol. XVI, no. 7, Oct. 1925.
3 G. H. Thomson, 'The Nature and Measurement of Intellect', *Teachers College Record*, vol. XLI, no. 8, May 1940.

argued (assuming the samples to be representative and numerically large enough) that these curves might not represent the actual distribution of intelligence in the grade, either because of the error attached to each individual score or because of the inequality of the units in each of the given tests. For example, if, as is possible, the errors attached to the individual scores are themselves normally distributed, then, whatever the actual distribution of intelligence, the distribution apparent from the observational results might have an appearance of normality. Thorndike found, however, that reducing the error attached to each individual measurement did not reduce the tendency (as measured by Pearson's χ^2 test) towards a normal distribution. He also argued that among the eleven tests inequalities in the units of one test in one direction would be balanced by like inequalities in the units of some other test in the opposite direction. He therefore combined the eleven separate distributions into one distribution by averaging the frequencies for each tenth of a standard deviation, and he found that a normal curve was practically a perfect fit for this combined distribution.[1] He therefore concluded that intelligence was normally distributed throughout the sixth grade.

This argument hardly appears to be justified. The view that the units of a given test may be unequal needs quite as much proof as the view that they are equal, in the sense that both views may be meaningless. If, as is possible, the

[1] See, however, the footnote on p. 729 in the article by Thomson previously quoted.

number attached to an individual by means of a test is a purely ordinal mark, then it is meaningless to talk about the units being either equal or unequal. For instead of the numbers attached we might as well have attached letters of the alphabet or any ordered set of symbols, and it is clearly meaningless to discuss such questions as whether the difference between a and b is equal or is unequal to the difference between f and g. Thus Thorndike's proof that intelligence is normally distributed in a given age group assumes that intelligence is measurable in some sense other than the sense appropriate to intensive magnitudes, and it cannot therefore be made the basis of an argument in defence of that proposition.

As far as I know there is no conclusive proof that intelligence is normally distributed throughout an age group, and indeed it is probable that such a proof could only be obtained after it has been shown that intelligence is measurable in a sense other than that appropriate to intensive magnitudes. But although there is no proof it is nevertheless possible, and, on the analogy of some physical characteristics, even probable that it is normally distributed, and we must therefore consider the remainder of the argument, which professes to show the sense in which intelligence can be measured on a scale of equal units. It should perhaps be noted that the sense of 'hereditary' in which it was suggested in the last chapter intelligence was hereditary, is the only one which gives much plausibility to the view that intelligence is normally distributed. If intelligence is transmitted in the first sense of 'hereditary' (that is, as a Mendelian character) it is almost certainly not normally distributed.

The remainder of the argument has been used in one form or another by many educationists. The essential step consists in transforming the percentages of a group which succeed at different levels into measures of deviation from the average of the group. This is done from tables of the normal curve, and the deviation is expressed in terms of sigma, the standard deviation, or some multiple of it. Thus the number which is now attached to each individual as the result of a test expresses the deviation of that individual from the average in terms of some unit which is related to the standard deviation of the population. It is claimed that such numbers are in a scale with equal units.

Such a claim is justified only if the above assumption is true, that is, only if the property tested is normally distributed throughout the population. When that is so then the argument affords a *definition* of what is meant by equal units. It is only a definition, for the argument makes no attempt to show that an experimental process exists which satisfies the conditions for fundamental measurement. It is the existence of such a process in the case of length which gives a meaning to addition and hence to equality of units. But in this argument equal units of the property to be measured have been defined by equal units of length measured along the base-line of a normal curve. There is, of course, no objection to such a definition provided it is clearly realized that all that has happened is that a definition has been introduced. The danger is that many educationists write as if the units were 'really equal', which implies that some process similar to that which exists for length had been discovered.

The position which we have reached so far is this. We have no conclusive evidence that intelligence is normally distributed, but if it is we can find units of intelligence that are equal by definition. But we have not found any process, and indeed it is unlikely that any process will ever be found, which enables us to say that the units are experimentally equal. It is therefore almost certain that intelligence (and also the other properties measured by educationists) cannot be measured in what has been called a fundamental sense.

We must then consider the last alternative, namely, that such properties can be measured as derived magnitudes. It seems to me to be extremely probable that some of these properties are derived magnitudes, but I do not think that we can claim that they have been proved to be so. It is the lack of such a proof, that is, the lack of any evidence that to each individual possessing the property may be assigned a number which occurs in a numerical law, that is the missing link in experimental education to-day. The nearest approach to such a law is, perhaps, that an individual's intelligence quotient remains constant throughout his life; it is not surprising that this result is considered to be one of the most important of those obtained by testers.

The remainder of this chapter will be devoted to the consideration of a number of other reasons all of which point to the necessity of discovering numerical laws.

It is perhaps instructive to consider by way of comparison the conception of temperature. The relation 'felt to be hotter than' generates an order among objects, and it was discovered at an early stage that an objective method of observing this relation was by means of a mercury-in-glass thermometer. Two fixed marks were made on the glass corresponding to the level of mercury when water boiled and when ice melted, and the intervening length was divided into one hundred equal parts. This division into equal lengths is completely arbitrary, and the numbers consequently attached to bodies to 'measure' temperature are purely ordinal marks, and measure temperature precisely in the same way as hardness is measured by Mohs's scale. The measurement of intelligence on the scale obtained by dividing the length of the base-line of the normal curve into equal parts is measurement in the same sense, and, as we have seen, must not be confused with fundamental measurement. As long as temperature was considered solely in this way the conception was not of much use in physics. No doubt it enabled people to judge easily whether one object was hotter than another, just as intelligence tests enable people to judge easily whether one individual is more intelligent than another. But progress was only made when it was found that there was a numerical law $p.v = \text{constant}$, where the constant is related to the former conception of temperature in the sense that the orders generated are the same. It is a law such as this that is required in educational measurement to-day.

The discovery of numerical laws is necessary, however, not only if progress is to be made, but also if many current practices are to have meaning. Thus the movement known as factor analysis consists of making certain calculations from sets of correlation coefficients. These correlation coefficients are generally calculated from the observed performances of individuals on the assumption that the variables are normally distributed.[1] Such an assumption has meaning only when the variables are measurable in some sense other than that appropriate to intensive magnitudes, and since it is almost certain they are not fundamental magnitudes the assumption is meaningful only when they are derived magnitudes. It should be understood, however, that, very probably, the assumption is not only meaningful but true, but it can be proved to be so only when numerical laws have been discovered. No doubt a number of spectacular practical successes obtained by the factorists would imply that the assumption was probably true, in accordance with the theorems of inverse probability, but it is precisely because the successes are not spectacular that it seems desirable to provide the movement with an adequate theoretical basis.

[1] If the variables are obviously not normally distributed it is assumed that the 'underlying theoretical distributions of test abilities are normal' (L. L. Thurstone, *Primary Mental Abilities*, p. 59).

There is another branch of the testing movement which is even more dependent on the discovery of numerical laws, and that is the branch concerned with the reliability of tests. Most educationists assume that the variables they are working with have a 'true value' which can be measured with a greater or less degree of accuracy. If the same test is given on two different occasions then the correlation between the two sets of results is said to measure the reliability of the test, and this is made use of in estimating the 'true value' of an individual's score. For example, if an individual scores 50 in a test of reliability 0·91 and standard deviation 10, then the probable error of his score can be calculated as

$$0·6745 \times 10 \times \sqrt{(1-0·91)} = 0·6745 \times 10 \times 0·3 = 2·0235,$$

which means that there is approximately an even chance that his true score lies between 48 and 52. The conceptions of 'errors' and of 'true values' in educational measurement are, I think, meaningless unless we assume the existence of numerical laws.

The theory of errors was developed largely to deal with astronomical observations, where what I have called the subjective conditions of measurement are specially important. But in educational measurements the subjective conditions ought not to cause any trouble. For it would be sheer carelessness on the part of the experimenter if the subjective conditions caused any inconsistent measures. The errors of measurement in education arise from two causes. First of all, it is possible that two individuals A and B may make the same score on a test T_1, and that B and C may make the same score on a second test T_2, while A and C will not make the same score on a third test T_3, where T_1, T_2 and T_3 all test the same property. This may be due to the fact that A may possess the property to a slightly greater extent than B, and B than C, but that the difference is so small that T_1 and T_2 are unable to discriminate between them, while T_3 can discriminate between A and C. In a similar way two weights P and Q may appear to balance as do also Q and R, while P and R do not. Physicists ascribe such inconsistencies to what is called the 'step' of the measuring instrument. Thus all instruments, including tests, have associated with them a certain margin of error, and this is true no matter how 'refined' the instrument may be. It arises from the fact that it is possible to have only a finite number of steps in any scale, and there is no reason why all the objects which are measured should coincide exactly with these steps.

The second cause of errors of measurement in education is that the properties which are measured in individuals vary from day to day. It seems strange that inconsistencies which arise from this cause should be called errors of measurement, for it is part of what is meant by measurement that the measure should alter when the property changes, and that the property has changed when the measure is found to be different. Nevertheless, educationists regard 'reliability' as a characteristic of the test or measuring instrument and not of the property which is being measured. This seems to me to be a mistake. If a process of assigning numbers to represent a property has been decided upon, then a different number must mean that the property measured by the test has changed.

If we compare the situation with what happens in physics I think we can perhaps find a solution. Suppose we make a number of measurements of the temperature of a gas. These will in general be found to be inconsistent, but the 'true value' of the temperature is that which is related to the pressure and volume by the well-known gas law, and it has no other meaning. Such a law is sometimes called an equation of condition, and there is a standard process of 'adjusting the observations to fit the equations of condition'. Similarly, the different measures obtained by the application of an educational test may be adjusted when an equation of condition, that is, a numerical law, is known. But until such a law is known the conception of 'true value' is meaningless.

I have no suggestions to make as to what a possible law in education might be. But some laws will have to be obtained. It may be urged that throughout this chapter I have assumed that measurement in education must be similar to measurement in physics and that such an assumption need not be true. But it is true. In the last few years we have seen how the borderline between physics and chemistry has been completely removed, and it is becoming increasingly clear that wherever measurement can be applied, there the methods of physics are appropriate.

Indeed physics can almost be defined as the science of measurement. It is here that the Behaviourists with their emphasis on the behavioural responses of the individual have made their most valuable contribution to educational psychology. If there is to be a science of educational measurement at all then these behavioural responses must be found to obey numerical laws, such that the constants occurring therein order the individuals in the same way as psychological properties. From the obvious health of educational research to-day it is not likely to be long before some such laws are discovered, and I have little doubt that they will be found to justify much of the work that has already been done.

INDEX

149

CAMBRIDGE: PRINTED BY WALTER LEWIS, M.A., AT THE UNIVERSITY PRESS